Praise For Hymns Of Note

William Long's enthusiasm for hymns is surpassed only by his knowledge of them... His books are a wonderful devotional and the perfect gift for a hymn lover.

Kerrie and Kellie – Hosts of the Hymn Talk Twin Talk podcast

Buying this book has been a blessing to me personally and my ministry.

Liz Dayspring - Gospel Artist and Author

I can think of many creative ways to use this book. Definitely include it with your daily devotions as a way to prepare your heart for God's Word.

Aaron Lee - @diveindigdeep, diveindigdeep.com

Good hymns have that profound ability to, at once, raise you up into the heavens and place your soul before the throne of grace in almost an instant. *Hymns of Note* performs that very function! *Hymns of Note* will be a wonderful addition to your library and I highly recommend adding this book to your personal times of devotion...

Matt Blair - Pilgrim Hymns

Hymns of Note would be a fantastic tool to aid any believer's personal or family devotions. If you teach or preach regularly, it would serve as a gold mine of illustrations that will help those you teach connect timeless truths to their lives.

Nick Minerva - Lead Pastor of Fresno Church

HYMNS OF NOTE

Rejoice

William Long

Also by William Long:

Hymns Of Note

For the people of
Hertford Baptist Church

My soul magnifies the Lord,
And my spirit rejoices
In God my Saviour

Luke 1:46-47

Contents

Hymns
In Chronological Order

Introduction
Hymns In A Time Of Crisis

I wrote *Hymns Of Note* in the summer of 2018 as a newly married man. My wife, Agnes, and I had just started a long and difficult struggle to challenge the refusal of her spousal visa, so that she could come and live with me in England. It was during those long eighteen months of waiting that the words of hymns, and the stories of their writers, spoke to me. It was like the scene in *Raiders of the Lost Ark* where Indiana Jones places the Staff of Ra on the ground in the tomb and a beam of light shines through the window, hits the gem on the head of the staff, and illuminates the location of the Ark of the Covenant on a model city of Cairo. God had shone a light on old hymns, knowing that I was going to need them.

I published *Hymns Of Note* in November 2020, almost a year after the start of the pandemic, and the response I received was phenomenal. 2020 was a difficult year for all of us, and many of the hymns I had selected were written after the hymnists had gone through their own difficult times. A whole group of people were now seeing these hymns in a new way. For many people they were encountering these hymns for the first time, whilst for others they were blowing the dust from these old hymns and seeing them in a new light.

I wrote the book you're currently holding in the summer of 2021. It was three years after I had written the first book and a year and a half after the UK had entered their first lockdown.

I'm inclined to say that we need hymns now more than ever, but I don't think that's true. I think we always need hymns, new and old, in times of joy and in times of sorrow, because singing to God is an integral part of a Christian faith. What I will say is that we need hymns now, as much as we ever have.

In *Hymns Of Note* I spoke about the hymns *It Is Well* and *Tis So Sweet To Trust In Jesus*. Both of these hymns were written after separate tragedies. *It Is Well* was written by Horatio Spafford after his daughters died when the ship they were travelling on was struck by another boat. *Tis So Sweet To Trust In Jesus* was written by Louisa Stead after she and her daughter watched her husband drown whilst trying to save a boy at the beach. In their mourning, and in the throws of sorrow and heartbreak, they turned to God and wrote these two hymns. (You can listen to me talk about *Tis So Sweet To Trust In Jesus* on episode 33 of the *Hymn Talk Twin Talk* podcast with the hosts Kerrie and Kellie.)

It is natural for us to turn to music in difficult times and it is different for each of us. Some people might like to listen to sad melancholic music that matches their mood so that they can process their feelings. Others prefer to look for joyful and uplifting music when they're feeling down to lift their spirits. My wife belongs to the first group of people, whilst I firmly belong to the second group.

David wrote many of his Psalms when he was facing trouble. In those times, when death felt looming and his enemies drew near, he turned to song. Psalm 27 is a perfect example of this. David starts by asking, *"...whom shall I fear?"* and then begins to list everything that he should be afraid of: evildoers assailing him to eat his flesh, armies encamping around him, and wars rising against him. Any one of these is enough to strike fear into our hearts, but not David. The reason for this comes in the first verse when he says, *"The Lord is my light and my salvation..."* and *"...The Lord is the stronghold of my life..."* David is facing death but he isn't afraid because he firmly understands who God is.

As David waits for the events to unfold around him he isn't blind to his circumstances but he can see more than the distressing nature of his situation. He can see God. And because of that he sings.

In his time of worship he prays that he may dwell in the house of the Lord and gaze upon His beauty. He acknowledges that God will be his shelter, and will conceal him from his enemies, and will lift him high upon a rock to keep him safe. He says:

> *And now my head shall be lifted up*
>   *above my enemies all around me,*
> *and I will offer in his tent*
>   *sacrifices with shouts of joy;*
> *I will sing and make melody to the Lord.*
> (Psalm 27:6)

In the midst of trouble, with war brewing around him, and his enemies drawing near, David is shouting for joy and singing praises to God, because God is keeping him safe. He ends his song full of hope, with strength, and with courage. He says:

> *I believe that I shall look upon the goodness of the Lord*
> *in the land of the living!*
> *Wait for the Lord;*
> *be strong, and let your heart take courage;*
> *wait for the Lord!*
> (Psalm 27:13-14)

He didn't wait until his enemies had been defeated, or until he was out of harms way, to sing to God. He sang to God in the midst of his troubles, and he did so with joy, strength, and courage.

In 2 Chronicles 20, Jehoshaphat and the people of Judah intended to conquer the city of Moab with a song. God sent his Holy Spirit to Jehoshaphat to tell him that the battle was not *theirs* to fight, but *God's*. He said, *"You will not need to fight in this battle... the Lord will be with you."* So Jehoshaphat gathered his army and appointed those who were to sing to God. He dressed them in holy attire and put the choir at the *front* of the army. They were on the front line, with neither shields nor swords, and they sang, *"Give thanks to the Lord, for his steadfast love endures forever."*

As they sang, God sent an ambush against their enemies and the three armies that were set to fight Judah killed each other. Even though the victory of the battle was God's, it was the singing of the choir that evoked the victory. If they hadn't sung they wouldn't have won.

American pastor John Piper says, *"Singing is not merely a response to grace. Singing is a means of grace. Singing is power. When you sing, the Holy Spirit comes and does something."*

Acts 16 recounts Paul and Silas praying and singing hymns to God in prison after they had been arrested. And when they sang, the prison shook like an earthquake, causing all of the prison doors to open and all of the shackles and bonds to fall off.

Life is full of difficulties and struggles. It isn't just expected that we'll face persecution but Jesus promised it (John 15:18). Sometimes we'll face troubles alone, and other times, as the pandemic has shown, everyone will face them together. During these times it is important that we sing, not because it is a nice or a comforting thing to do, but because when we sing hymns to God, there is power.

When *you* sing hymns to God, there is power.

So now come, let us sing.

William Long
Hertford, 2021

Note

I have tried to use the original lyrics to the hymns but, as there are so many variations and minor differences between published versions, some may not be the author's original text. Where it was difficult to identify the original I chose the version that I felt best represented the author's intent.

Hymns

John Mason Neale

O Come O Come Emmanuel

8thC & 1861

Words

Anonymous

Translation

John Mason Neale

O come, O come, Emmanuel,
And ransom captive Israel;
That mourns in lonely exile here,
Until the Son of God appear.
Rejoice! Rejoice! Emmanuel
Shall come to Thee, O Israel!

O come, Thou Rod of Jesse, free
Thine own from Satan's tyranny;
From depths of hell Thy people save,
And give them victory o'er the grave.
Rejoice! Rejoice! Emmanuel
Shall come to Thee, O Israel!

O come, Thou Day-Spring, come and cheer
Our spirits by Thine Advent here;
Disperse the gloomy clouds by night,
And death's dark shadows put to flight.
Rejoice! Rejoice! Emmanuel
Shall come to Thee, O Israel!

O come, Thou Key of David, come,
And open wide our heavenly home;
Make safe the way that leads on high,
And close the path to misery.
Rejoice! Rejoice! Emmanuel
Shall come to Thee, O Israel!

O come, O come, Thou Lord of might!
Who to thy tribes, on Sinai's height,
In ancient times didst give the law,
In cloud, and majesty, and awe.
Rejoice! Rejoice! Emmanuel
Shall come to Thee, O Israel!

Therefore the Lord himself will give you a sign. Behold, the virgin shall conceive and bear a son, and shall call his name Immanuel.

Isaiah 7:14

O Come O Come Emmanuel originated as an ancient advent hymn. It is believed to have been written around the 8th Century and was originally written in Latin. It is a paraphrase of the *Great Advent Antiphons*, a chant based upon Mary's the Magnificat from Luke 1:46-55. Antiphons were chanted and sung by monks during their evening prayers. The *Great Advent Antiphons* were sung specifically during advent, in the seven-day lead-up to Christmas. The monks would sing a single verse each day, in anticipation of Christmas Eve, and then on Christmas Eve they would also sing the Magnificat.

The author of the original Latin text had a great scriptural understanding of Christ's arrival. Not only is each verse its own individual prayer, welcoming Jesus' arrival, but they are ordered in such a way that, in Latin, the titles of Christ form an acrostic composition, which spells the phrase '*I will come tomorrow.*' The monks weren't just praying for Jesus' arrival each day, they were also praying a week-long prayer that concluded on Christmas Eve.

In 1861, John M. Neale translated the text into English. Neale was a priest and scholar from London, England. He studied at Trinity College,

Cambridge, where he became the best classics scholar in his year. He wrote many original hymns, and published collections of hymns for children, but his greatest contribution were the numerous hymns he translated from Greek and Latin into English. He never claimed the rights to his work because he wanted his translations to belong to Christians everywhere.

Christmas is anticipated in many ways. Some people have advent calendars, some people may light advent candles, and others may have their own traditions that are unique to their family. There's a lot preparation to be done. There are presents to be wrapped, a tree to be decorated, cookies to be baked... But the *heart* of advent is anticipation. Many people say that they prefer Christmas Eve to Christmas Day because of how exciting the build up is.

Whilst we have modern distractions that keep us from focusing on the true meaning of Christmas, the monks who sang the original Latin hymn had their own distractions and used the hymn as a way to focus their minds on Christ's arrival.

Each of Christ's titles that start the verses are taken from the Old Testament. It is a beautiful reminder that, as we anticipate the coming of Christmas, people had been anticipating the arrival of the Christ for thousands of years before Jesus came.

So when we sing *O Come, O Come Emmanuel* in our Christmas services we're taking part in an ancient tradition of anticipating Christ's arrival, only as modern worshipers we don't have to wonder what our saviour will be like or what he will do. We know exactly who Emmanuel is and what his arrival accomplished so during the Christmas season we can personally and whole-heartedly celebrate.

O come, O come, Emmanuel

Kolbeinn Tumason

Hear, Smith Of Heavens

1208

Words

Kolbeinn Tumason

Translation

Anonymous

Music

Þorkell Sigurbjörnsson

Hear, smith of heavens,
what the poet asks.
May softly come unto me
thy mercy.
So I call on thee,
for thou hast created me.
I am thy slave,
thou art my Lord.

God, I call on thee
to heal me.
Remember me, mild one,
Most we need thee.
Drive out, O king of suns,
generous and great,
human every sorrow
from the fortress of the heart.

Watch over me, mild one,
Most we need thee,
truly every moment
in the world of men.
send us, son of the virgin,
good causes,
all aid is from thee,
in my heart.

Hear a just cause, O Lord; attend to my cry!
Give ear to my prayer from lips free of deceit!
From your presence let my vindication come!
Let your eyes behold the right!

Psalm 17:1-2

Hear Smith Of Heavens is one of Iceland's most famous hymns and the events that led to it being written are fascinating.

Medieval Iceland was ruled by mighty family clans. One of the most powerful clans was the Ásbirnings. They dominated northern Iceland during the 12th and 13th Centuries. Each district of the Icelandic Commonwealth were led by chieftains, who were responsible for making decisions regarding their clan, and also acted as judges. Kolbeinn Tumason of the Ásbirnings, born in 1173, was the most powerful chieftain in northern Iceland.

As a way to cement power, Kolbeinn would appoint people he trusted into high positions within the church. Even though Christianity had been introduced to Iceland long before the Vikings arrived in around 870, the Catholic Church was relatively new and had only been in Iceland for around 200 years. One of the men Kolbeinn appointed was his wife's uncle, Gudmund Arasson, who was serving as a priest at the time. Kolbeinn promoted Gudmund to a bishop. Kolbeinn expected Gudmund to be devoted to him and his morals, but instead Gudmund strove to make the church more powerful in Iceland, and tried to diminish the power of secular chieftains such as Kolbeinn. He believed that the church should be its own entity, free of interference from those outside of the church. Kolbeinn had not expected this turn of events and a rivalry was formed.

Over the next few years, tensions grew between them. Kolbeinn acted as a judge against a number of Gudmunds priests. Gudmund refused to give up any of his men to the secular judges. He wanted these matters within the church to be dealt with within the church. This all came to a head when Kolbeinn's men arrested one of Gudmund's priests who had been accused of abusing a woman. As a result he forbade any of his priests from being of service to Kolbeinn in any way.

In 1208 the escalation of their conflict resulted in what is now known as the Battle of Víðines. Kolbeinn's troops fought against Gudmund's troops, fighting for power. Kolbeinn was killed in battle. His head was caved in by a large rock.

Kolbeinn wrote *Hear, Smith Of Heavens* before entering the battle. He wrote it as prayer to God. He starts the first verse by asking God to hear him, and to listen to his prayer, in the same way that David does in his Psalms. He then offers himself to God, calling himself a slave, and asks for mercy. In the second verse he asks God to heal him, to remember him, and to cast out the sorrows from his heart. He finishes the hymn with the third verse, where he prays for God to watch over him and he acknowledges that all help he has received has come from God.

Kolbeinn was clearly a knowledgeable man, and one who was educated in his faith. So much of his hymn seems to echo the Psalms David wrote whilst he was being pursued by his enemies. Although Kolbeinn's nemesis was a bishop, he wasn't fighting against God, he was fighting against the corruption he saw in the church. Even though he acted as what Gudmund called a secular chieftain, he led his clan in a way he thought was right, and fought for justice, all the while praying to God for guidance. And before facing the biggest battle of his life, which unbeknownst to him would be his last, he took the time to pray, and to worship God, for he knew that there was nothing he could achieve without the help of The Smith of the Heavens.

Hear,
Smith of Heavens,
What the poet asks

Francis Rous

The Lord's My Shepherd

1650

Words

Francis Rous

Music

Jessie Seymour Irvine

The Lord's my shepherd, I'll
  not want.
He makes me down to lie
In pastures green: he leadeth me
the quiet waters by.

My soul he doth restore again;
and me to walk doth make
Within the paths of righteousness,
ev'n for his own name's sake.

Yea, though I walk in death's
  dark vale,
yet will I fear none ill:
For thou art with me; and thy rod
and staff me comfort still.

My table thou hast furnished
in presence of my foes;
My head thou dost with
  oil anoint,
and my cup overflows.

Goodness and mercy all my life
shall surely follow me:
And in God's house for evermore
my dwelling-place shall be.

The Lord is my shepherd; I shall not want. He makes me lie down in green pastures. He leads me beside still waters.

Psalm 23:1-2

Francis Rous was born in Devon in 1579. He was a politician and a devout Puritan who, for a brief period, became Speaker of the House of Commons. At the time, many people believed that there should be a universal church and every church should follow the exact same structures and practices as decided by a single governing body. The Church of England had been founded only 45 years earlier and many people disagreed on what the structure of a universal church should take. Rous's Puritanism meant that instead of forming a universal church he wanted to reform and purify the Church of England.

Rous had a long career as a member of parliament, which started in 1626 when he became a Member of Parliament (MP) for Truro, in Cornwall, and then became an MP for Tregony two years later. Whilst he was an MP, there was wide-spread belief in the divine right of Kings and their appointment by God. MP's believed that this undermined the role of Parliament. Rous made a speech in which he condemned the belief that the King had been appointed by God. King Charles I responded by dissolving Parliament, making himself an unaccountable ruler.

This led to the English Civil War, which saw Royalists, led by King Charles I, fighting against Parliamentarians, which included Oliver Cromwell and Francis Rous.

It was during the English Civil War that Rous wrote and published *The Psalms of David set forth in English Meeter*. It was a collection of Psalms that Rous had paraphrased to fit the poetic metre, or rhythmic structure, of English poetry. Rous's paraphrasing meant that the Psalms could be comfortably sung to the melodies of popular hymns. After publication, his text for *The Lord's My Shepherd* was heavily edited into the more common version we sing today.

The Lord's My Shepherd is paraphrased from Psalm 23, which David likely wrote later on in his life. In the Psalm, David remembers his time as a shepherd and realised that God's nature was similar to that of a shepherd. He knew that sheep could trust and follow their shepherd because they would lead them to green pastures, water, and a place to rest, and would protect them from danger. David decided to let God lead him, and submitted himself to God like a sheep to their shepherd, knowing that he'd be looked after and protected.

The English Civil War was a dangerous, complicated and uncertain time. *The Lord's My Shepherd* reveals that Rous knew how important it was to let God take the lead as Rous walked through his own dark vale.

John Newton (young)

The Lord Will Provide

1775

Words
John Newton

Music
John Roberts

Tho' troubles assail, and dangers affright,
Tho' friends should all fail, and foes all unite;
Yet one thing secures us, whatever betide,
The promise assures us, The Lord will provide.

The birds without barn and storehouse are fed;
From them let us learn to trust for our bread:
His saints what is fitting shall ne'er be deny'd,
So long as it's written, The Lord will provide.

We may, like the ships, by tempests be tost
On perilous deeps, but need not be lost:
Tho' Satan enrages the wind and the tide,
Yet scripture engages, The Lord will provide.

His call we'll obey, like Abra'm of old;
We know not the way, but faith makes us bold;
For tho' we are strangers, we have a good guide,
And trust in all dangers, The Lord will provide.

When Satan appears to stop up our path,
And fills us with fears, we triumph by faith:
He cannot take from us (tho' oft he has try'd)
The heart-cheering promise, The Lord will provide.

He tells us we're weak, our hope is in vain,
The good that we seek, we ne'er shall obtain;
But when such suggestions our graces have try'd
This answers all questions, The Lord will provide.

No strength of our own, nor goodness we claim,
Our trust is all thrown on Jesus's name;
In this our strong tower for safety we hide;
The Lord is our power, The Lord will provide.

When life sinks apace, and death is in view,
The word of his grace shall comfort us through;
Not fearing nor doubting with Christ on our side,
We hope to die shouting, The Lord will provide.

Abraham said, "God will provide for himself the lamb for a burnt offering, my son." So they went both of them together.

Genesis 22:8

John Newton, the writer of *Amazing Grace*, wrote *The Lord Will Provide* in 1775 and published it in 1779 as part of the *Olney Hymns*. Newton published the *Olney Hymns* with his friend and poet, William Cowper (who you can read about in *Hymns of Note*) for his rural parish of Olney. Newton wanted to curate a collection of hymns that his parishioners, most of whom were poor and uneducated, could easily understand and sing, and that would give them a stronger understanding of who God is.

The Lord Will Provide is all about the generosity of God's provisions. It is rich in Biblical theology, and each verse builds upon the theme with multiple Biblical references.

The first verse is about how fleeting friends can be and how strong our enemies appear. These are references to Psalms 88 and 94:

> *You have caused my beloved and my friend to shun me;*
> *my companions have become darkness.* (Psalm 88:18)

> *They band together against the life of the righteous*
> *and condemn the innocent to death.* (Psalm 94:21)

The second verse talks about how God looks after the birds of the air, even though they do not have barns to store their feed. This mirrors Jesus' words in Matthew 6:26, when he said:

> *"Look at the birds of the air: they neither sow nor reap nor gather into barns, and yet your heavenly Father feeds them. Are you not of more value than they?"*

Each verse ends with the same line: *'The Lord will provide'*. These are similar to the words spoken by Abraham after God tested him by commanding him to sacrifice his son, Isaac. Abraham took Isaac to the land of Moriah, where he took him to the top of a mountain. Isaac asked his father why they had fire and wood but no lamb for the burnt offering. Abraham replied, *"God will provide for himself the lamb for a burnt offering, my son."* (Genesis 22:8) and then in Genesis 22:14 it is revealed that Abraham named that place on the mountain *The Lord Will Provide*.

Through the hymn, John Newton was able to teach his congregation to rely on God. As a poor community they would have faced money worries, and had their own fears and concerns for the future. Newton used this hymn to show them that they can trust God to provide for them, and that no matter how dire their situations were, they could have hope that the Lord would provide for them. Newton uses examples and promises from the Bible, along with the repetition of the final line of each verse, to really drive the point home. He's essentially saying, "The Lord will provide, and here is all of the evidence that proves it."

The promise assures us, The Lord will provide

Joachim Neander

Praise To The Lord, The Almighty

1680

Words

Joachim Neander

Translation

Catherine Winkworth

Music

Anonymous

Praise to the Lord! the Almighty, the King of creation!
O my soul, praise Him, for He is thy health and salvation!
All ye who hear,
Now to His temple draw near,
Join me in glad adoration!

Praise to the Lord! who o'er all things so wondrously reigneth,
Shelters thee under His wings, yea so gently sustaineth;
Hast thou not seen
How thy desires have been
Granted in what He ordaineth?

Praise to the Lord! who doth prosper thy work and defend thee,
Surely His goodness and mercy here daily attend thee;
Ponder anew
What the Almighty can do,
If with His love He befriend thee!

Praise to the Lord! Oh let all that is in me adore Him!

All that hath life and breath, come now with praises before Him!

Let the Amen

Sound from His people again,

Gladly for aye we adore Him!

Bless the Lord, O my soul,
  and all that is within me,
    bless his holy name!
Bless the Lord, O my soul,
  and forget not all his benefits,
who forgives all your iniquity,
  who heals all your diseases,
who redeems your life from the pit,
  who crowns you with steadfast love and mercy,
who satisfies you with good
  so that your youth is renewed like the eagle's.

Psalm 103:1-5

Joachim Neander, a Calvinist schoolmaster, wrote the original German text of *Praise To The Lord, The Almighty*, in 1680. It was the year he died. He died when he was only thirty, after contracting tuberculosis. Despite dying at a young age, Neander became one of the most important hymnists of the German church, and wrote around 60 hymns. Many of his hymns were jubilant songs, full of praise and thanksgiving. He loved to celebrate God's creation of nature and the beauty of His works.

After studying theology, and being influenced by Philipp Spener, a Lutheran theologian and Father of Pietism, Neander became a Pietist himself. He believed that putting his trust in Jesus Christ was the foundation and centre of their faith, rather than theological philosophies, which was the emphasis of the Lutheran church at the time.

The words to his hymn, *Praise To The Lord*, reflect the beliefs of a man who isn't bogged down by complex theology, but can rejoice in the simple truth of his faith: God is the King of creation, so I'm going to praise Him.

The hymn is based on Psalms 103 and 150. Psalm 103 opens with *'Bless the Lord, O my soul,'* and goes on to list the greatness of God's character and the things he has done. Psalm 150 opens with *'Praise the Lord!'*, and then lists the instruments that we should praise him with: the trumpet, lute, harp, tambourine, cymbals. Its final line, *'Let everything that has breath praise the Lord! Praise the Lord!'* Is emphasised in the final verse of the hymn, *'All that hath life and breath, come now with praises before Him!'*

Almost two hundred years after Neander wrote the hymn, it was translated into English by Catherine Winkworth. Winkworth was born in London, England in 1827. She translated a huge amount of hymns from German into English. She lived in Dresden, Germany with relatives for a year and became fascinated by German hymns. Wanting to bring these hymns to England, she embarked on a mission to translate as many as she could. She'd often alter them slightly to match sensibilities of her time. For instance, in Neander's original text, the second line of the first verse reflects Psalm 150's call to praise God with Psalter and harp, which was popular in German Renaissance hymn writing. Winkworth changed this line to put an emphasis on health and salvation, which was a more common theme for 19th-century Christianity.

I think it's fitting to mention that, after his death, Neander had a valley named after him. Neandertal, or the Neander Valley, is located East of Düsseldorf, where Neander wrote most of his hymns. Two centuries after his death, a skull was discovered in a limestone quarry in Neandertal. It was the first known discovery of a Homo Neanderthalensis, more commonly known as a Neanderthal. The name Neander means 'new man', so it is more than appropriate that this discovery of a new species of man was named after Joachim Neander, a man who loved his creator and all of His creations.

Nahum Tate

While Shepherds Watched Their Flocks

1700

Words

Nahum Tate

Music

George Kirbye

While Shepherds watch'd their Flocks
    by Night,
all seated on the Ground,
The Angel of the Lord came down,
And Glory shone around.
"Fear not," said he (for mighty Dread
had seiz'd their troubled Mind,)
"Glad Tidings of great Joy I bring
to you and all Mankind."

"To you in David's town this Day
is born of David's Line,
The Saviour who is Christ
    the Lord;
And this shall be the sign:
The heav'nly babe, you there
    shall find
To human view display'd,
All meanly wrapt in swathing bands,
And in a manger laid."

Thus spake the seraph, and
    forthwith
Appear'd a shining throng
Of Angels praising God, and thus
addrest their joyful Song:
"All Glory be to God on High;
and to the Earth be Peace;
Good-will henceforth from
    Heav'n to Men
begin and never cease."

And in the same region there were shepherds out in the field, keeping watch over their flock by night. And an angel of the Lord appeared to them, and the glory of the Lord shone around them, and they were filled with great fear. And the angel said to them, "Fear not, for behold, I bring you good news of great joy that will be for all the people. For unto you is born this day in the city of David a Savior, who is Christ the Lord.

Luke 2:8-11

Before the 1700's, the only songs that were allowed to be sung within the Anglican Church were the Psalms of David. The Psalms were set to music, and sometimes versified. This changed in 1700 when Nahum Tate, who was England's Poet Laureate at the time, adapted the encounter that the shepherds had with the angels in Luke 2 and turned it into a hymn.

Nahum Tate was born in Dublin, Ireland, in 1692, and was the son of an Irish priest. Tate studied at Trinity College, Dublin, before moving to England to pursue a career in writing. It was whilst he was studying at Trinity College, in 1692, that he was made the third Poet Laureate of England by King William III and Queen Mary II.

Four years after he became Poet Laureate, Tate collaborated with the poet Nicholas Brady on *New Version of the Psalms of David*, which was a collection of metrical translations of the Psalms. They adapted the psalms into English musical metres so that they could be sung to the tunes that were common in England at the time. Tate wrote *While Shepherds Watched Their Flocks* to be included in a 1703 supplement for *New Version of the Psalms of David* and became the first hymn to be sung in the Anglican Church that wasn't directly from the book of Psalms.

It was a pinnacle moment in church history as it paved the way for more hymnists and writers to write their own hymns and in doing so they were able to move away from the Old Testament themes and imagery and introduce Jesus and gospel truths into their songs. To a modern church, it seems strange that they weren't singing about Jesus until then. After all, Jesus is the cornerstone of the church and the Christian faith. The fact that we now do sing songs about Jesus is, in part, thanks to the work of Nahum Tate.

While Shepherds Watched Their Flocks, is paraphrased from Luke 2:8-14. It focuses on the appearance of the angels to the shepherds when they announced to them the birth of Jesus. In the hymn, the story is retold simply but faithfully.

At the time, literacy was commonly restricted to men from the noble classes. As few as thirty percent of the population might have been able to read. Songs sung during church services often utilised calls and responses. The priest would sing the first line and the congregation would repeat it, so that those who couldn't read the lyrics could still sing along. The simple retelling of Luke's account of the shepherds meant that those who were unable to read could easily memorise and recount this favourite Christmas story, ensuring that the gospel was accessible for everyone.

Charles Wesley

And Can It Be

1738

Words

Charles Wesley

Music

Thomas Campbell

And can it be that I should gain
An int'rest in the Saviour's blood?
Died he for me, who caus'd his pain?
For me who him to death pursued?
Amazing love! how can it be,
That thou, my Lord, shouldst die
  for me?
Amazing love! how can it be,
That thou, my Lord, shouldst die
  for me?

'Tis mist'ry all, th' Immortal dies!
Who can explore his strange design?
In vain the first-born seraph tries
To sound the depths of love divine;
'Tis mercy all! let earth adore:
Let angel minds inquire no more.
Amazing love! how can it be,
That thou, my Lord, shouldst die
  for me?

He left his Father's throne above;
(So free, so infinite his grace!)
Emptied himself of all but love,
And bled for Adam's helpless race;
'Tis mercy all, immense and free,
For, O my God, it found out me!
Amazing love! how can it be,
That thou, my Lord, shouldst die
  for me?

Long my imprisoned spirit lay
Fast bound in sin and nature's night:
Thine eye diffused a quick'ning ray;
I woke: the dungeon flam'd
  with light;
My chains fell off, my heart was free--
I rose, went forth, and followed thee.
Amazing love! how can it be,
That thou, my Lord, shouldst die
  for me?

No condemnation now I dread;
Jesus, with all in him, is mine;
Alive in Him my living Head,
And clothed in righteousness divine,
Bold I approach th' eternal throne
And claim the crown, thro' Christ
   my own.
Amazing love! how can it be,
That thou, my Lord, shouldst die
   for me?

There is therefore now no condemnation for those
who are in Christ Jesus.

Romans 8:1

Charles Wesley wrote over 6500 hymns in his lifetime. He was born in 1707 in Lincolnshire, England. His older brother, John Wesley, was the founder of the Methodist movement, so Charles Wesley joined him and became one of the movement's leaders.

Wesley felt that he could express his thoughts and ideas best through hymns. He wrote hymns on just about everything, including his marriage, the rumoured French invasion, Christian festivals, stories from scripture, and the deaths of his loved ones and friends. *And Can It Be* was Wesley's way of processing and expressing his Christian faith after his miraculous conversion.

In May of 1738, Wesley was staying at the home of John Bray, in London, to recover his health. He was struggling with his breathing. Wesley heard a voice say, *"In the name of Jesus of Nazareth, arise, and believe, and thou shalt be healed of all thy infirmities."*

The words stirred Wesley's heart and convicted him. Later, Bray told him that his sister had felt compelled to say those words to him by God. Wesley jumped out of bed, opened his Bible, and found himself reading Psalm 40, which said to him:

He put a new song in my mouth,
a song of praise to our God.
Many will see and fear,
and put their trust in the Lord.

Wesley then wrote in his journal, *"I now found myself at peace with God, and rejoiced in the hope of a loving Christ."*

And Can It Be opens with a rhetorical question:

And can it be that I should gain
An int'rest in the Saviour's blood?

Wesley is asking if he can gain the great reward of Christ's crucifixion and resurrection if he was part of the reason Jesus had to die. Each verse ends with the same two lines:

Amazing love! how can it be,
That thou, my Lord, shouldst die for me?

Wesley is awestruck by God's love. He cannot believe that the God he worships, the maker of the universe, would lay down his life for him.

In the second verse, Wesley expresses his amazement at how God, who is immortal, could possibly die. He writes of the angels longing to look into the mystery of salvation, as Peter wrote in 1 Peter 1:12. Wesley comes to the conclusion that it is all because of God's mercy.

Wesley ends the hymn with an understanding that, now he is in Christ Jesus, there is no condemnation for him (Romans 8:1). He imagines himself approaching the throne of God and claiming the crown of life (James 1:12), now that he has Jesus Christ as his saviour.

The final verse closes with the same refrain as the previous verses. It's Wesley's way of expressing the almost absurdity that the God of the universe would lay down his own life for him:

> *Amazing Love! How can it be,*
> *That thou, my Lord, shouldst die for me?*

John Newton (older)

Amazing Grace

1779

Words

John Newton

Music

Anonymous

Amazing grace! How sweet the sound
That sav'd a wretch like me!
I once was lost, but now am found,
Was blind, but now I see.

'Twas grace that taught my heart
  to fear,
And grace my fears reliev'd;
How precious did that grace appear
The hour I first believ'd!

Thro' many dangers, toils, and snares,
I have already come;
'Tis grace hath brought me safe
  thus far,
And grace will lead me home.

The Lord has promis'd good to me,
His word my hope secures;
He will my shield and portion be,
As long as life endures.

Yes, when this flesh and heart
  shall fail,
And mortal life shall cease;
I shall possess within the veil,
A life of joy and peace.

The earth shall soon dissolve
  like snow,
The sun forbear to shine;
But God, who call'd me here below,
Will be forever mine.

For by grace you have been saved through faith. And this is not your own doing; it is the gift of God, not a result of works, so that no one may boast.

Ephesians 2:8-9

Amazing Grace is perhaps the anthem of Christians everywhere. Its words and tune are so prevalent and loved by many around the world that it might very well be the most famous hymn of all time, or even the most famous song of all time.

Its author, John Newton, had a difficult childhood. He was born in London, England in 1725, to a Christian family. When he was just six years old his mother contracted tuberculosis and died. Because his father was a shipping merchant and spent most of his time at sea, Newton went to live with his emotionally detached stepmother. He was later sent off to a boarding school, where he was terribly mistreated and became disenfranchised with authority, repeatedly acting out against it. When he was eleven years old, he went to work with his father on a ship at sea. After six voyages with him, his father retired and made plans for Newton to work in Jamaica on a sugarcane plantation. Newton rebelled, and instead signed on with a merchant ship that was sailing to the Mediterranean.

A year later, in 1743, whilst he was visiting friends, Newton was captured and forcefully conscripted to join the Royal Navy. Newton didn't want to be in the Navy and tried to dessert but was caught and punished in front of 350 of his fellow crew. He was stripped naked, whipped eight dozen times, and was then demoted.

Humiliated, Newton plotted to murder the captain as retribution, and then commit suicide by throwing himself overboard. After Newton's body healed from the whipping, and he had time to process his emotions, he decided instead to transfer to another ship. His new ship, called Pegasus, was a slave ship heading to West Africa to trade goods for slaves, before taking them to the Caribbean and North America. Newton didn't get on with the crew of the Pegasus, either. The crew decided to leave him in West Africa with Amos Clowe, a slave dealer, who gave him to his wife, Princess Peye of the Sherbro people, to be her servant. She mistreated and abused Newton as much as she did her slaves.

In 1745, Newton's father asked a sea captain to search for his son. The sea captain found and rescued Newton in West Africa and took him aboard his ship, the Greyhound. It was on this ship, and the voyage back to England, that Newton established his faith in God.

One night, Newton awoke to find that the Greyhound was caught in an awful storm off of the coast of Ireland. The boat was almost certainly about to sink. In his panic, Newton prayed to God. He begged for God's mercy and prayed that God would quell the storm. God answered his prayer. The storm settled and the Greyhound made it to port in one piece. His experience transformed him and he turned his life around, committing it to God.

After retiring from the slave trade, Newton published a pamphlet titled *Thoughts Upon the Slave Trade* where he described the terrible conditions that slaves were forced to endure. In it he apologised and said,

> *"It will always be a subject of humiliating reflection to me, an active instrument in a business at which my heart now shudders."*

Newton became an ally of William Wilberforce, the leader of the Parliamentary campaign to end slavery, and nine years later he saw the passing of the Slave Trade Act, which prohibited the slave trade in the British Empire.

When Newton reflected on his time working in the slave trade he came to the conclusion that his true Christian conversion must have come years after he originally thought it had. He argues that someone with a true belief in Jesus could not have continued to work in a trade that treated any human being as unworthy of God's love.

The words of *Amazing Grace* shine brighter when you consider the life that Newton lived before he wrote the hymn. The lyrics reveal the broken man that Newton was, and the man he would become. It is a moving and personal testament to the grace of God. The hymn becomes so much more powerful when you understand that the amazing grace that Newton received was as a result of him repenting for his work in the slave trade. It wasn't a fleeting grace that provided a small amount of comfort. It was *God's* grace and God's grace can free anyone from a lifetime of evil.

How precious did that grace appear the hour I first believ'd!

Edward Boatner

I Shall Not Be Moved

19th C

Words

Anonymous

Music

Traditional African
American Spiritual

Jesus keeps forever,
I shall not be moved;
He forsakes, no, never,
I shall not be moved;
Just like a tree that's planted by
the water,
I shall not be moved.

I shall not be, I shall not be moved,
I shall not be, I shall not be moved;
Just like a tree that's planted by
the water,
I shall not be moved.

On His strength depending,
I shall not be moved;
And His cause defending,
I shall not be moved;
Just like a tree that's planted by
the water,
I shall not be moved.

His, the love enfolding,
I shall not be moved;
His, the grace upholding,
I shall not be moved;
Just like a tree that's planted by
the water,
I shall not be moved.

Friend so high and holy,
I shall not be moved;
Friend so meek and lowly,
I shall not be moved;
Just like a tree that's planted by
the water,
I shall not be moved.

From the Bible story
I shall not be moved;
Living for His glory,
I shall not be moved;
Just like a tree that's planted by
  the water,
I shall not be moved.

With the faithful going,
I shall not be moved;
All His goodness knowing,
I shall not be moved;
Just like a tree that's planted by
  the water,
I shall not be moved.

By His truth I'm standing,
I shall not be moved;
Doing His commanding,
I shall not be moved;
Just like a tree that's planted by
  the water,
I shall not be moved.

I have set the Lord always before me: because he is at my right hand, I shall not be moved.

Psalm 16:8 KJV

I Shall Not Be Moved belongs to a genre of songs known as Spirituals. Spirituals have their roots in the transatlantic slave trade and their creation solely belongs to the generations of African Americans who were brought to America. The songs mixed cultural themes and the experience of being forced into slavery with traditional African musical techniques to create an entirely new genre.

Spirituals form the foundation of both gospel and blues music. They were often sung by slaves whilst they worked and laboured away. The content of the songs often reflected this hardship and their struggles, as well as connecting to scripture and biblical stories.

It's nigh on impossible to attribute spiritual songs to their African American authors. Many of them come from the oral tradition of passing on music and songs by singing them, and were rarely written down. And before the American Civil War these songs weren't documented and care wasn't taken to give credit to African American authors for their song writing. After the Civil War it became much more common place, and is easier to find the authors of post-war Spirituals. But there are countless songs whose origins and authors are lost to history.

It is assumed that *I Shall Not Be Moved* was sung as a pre-war slave song but there is no evidence that it was published before 1906 when Alfred Henry Ackley, a writer from Pennsylvania, collected and reworked African American Spirituals for publication. There is a version attributed to an African American composer called Edward Boatner, who published his version in 1929.

I Shall Not Be Moved is based on several pieces of scripture. The line *'Just like a tree that's planted by the water'* is taken from Jeremiah 17:7-8, which says:

> *"Blessed is the man who trusts in the Lord,*
> *whose trust is the Lord.*
> *He is like a tree planted by water,*
> *that sends out its roots by the stream,*
> *and does not fear when heat comes,*
> *for its leaves remain green,*
> *and is not anxious in the year of drought,*
> *for it does not cease to bear fruit."*

The song takes this Old Testament verse and updates it for the New Testament. It now says that it is *because* we trust in Jesus that we are like a tree planted by water. We don't have to fear and we do not need to be anxious.

The line *'I shall not be moved'* appears three times in each verse, and three times in the chorus. By the end of the song, if you sing all seven verses, you would have sung that line 42 times. This line is based on Psalm 16:8, which says:

> *I have set the Lord always before me: because he is at my right hand,*
> *I shall not be moved. (KJV)*

I Shall Not Be Moved is a declaration that we will be safe and secure, that we will not be afraid, and that we will be protected by God. The writer, and those who sing the song, are proclaiming that during the hardest parts of their life, and whatever hardships they might face, they are steadfast in the love of God and have a secure future with Christ as their saviour.

The African American slave, or slaves, who originally wrote this song faced tremendous hardships, and suffered a great amount, but, through it all, they could not be moved in their faith. No amount of evil or suffering that they faced in their day-to-day life could sway them in their faith in Jesus. They were firmly planted trees, with their roots drinking from the spring of living water, and, as the Spirituals prove, they absolutely could not be moved.

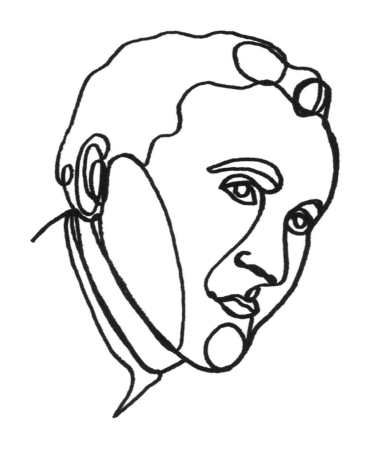

Joseph Mohr

Silent Night

1818

Words

Joseph Mohr

Translation

John Freeman Young
& Anonymous

Music

Franz Xaver Gruber

Silent night! holy night!
All is calm, all is bright,
Round yon virgin mother and child!
Holy Infant, so tender and mild,
Sleep in heavenly peace,
Sleep in heavenly peace.

Silent night! holy night!
Shepherds quake at the sight.
Glories stream from heaven afar,
Heavenly hosts sing, Hallelujah!
Christ, the Saviour, is born!
Christ, the Saviour, is born!

Silent night! holy night!
Son of God, love's pure light
Radiant beams from Thy holy face,
With the dawn of redeeming grace,
Jesus, Lord, at Thy birth.
Jesus, Lord, at Thy birth.

And she gave birth to her firstborn son and wrapped him in swaddling cloths and laid him in a manger, because there was no place for them in the inn.

Luke 2:7

Silent Night is the most popular Christmas carol in the world. Its popularity has spread all over the world and, even though it was written over 200 years ago, its popularity hasn't dwindled. If an artist is recording a Christmas album, it's more than likely that they'll have a rendition of *Silent Night* on there somewhere. Its modest tune makes it easy to adapt into almost any genre of music, and you can find renditions of *Silent Night* in a traditional gospel style, as well as a more alternative heavy metal style, and even modern electronica styles. Whatever the genre, for Christians and non-Christians, it sets the tone for a quiet, peaceful and nostalgic Christmas.

For such a global, well-loved hymn, it might be surprising to know that *Silent Night* has rather humble beginnings. It began in a small mountain town, in the Austrian countryside.

It was originally written by Joseph Mohr in German in 1816. He was the priest of a town called Mariapfarr. The Napoleonic Wars, which lasted for twelve years, had brought chaos to Austria. Their political system, and social infrastructure (such as hospitals, schools, and other public facilities) were devastated, and Mohr's congregation were suffering from the consequences.

Not only had the war overwhelmed Mohr's congregation, but in 1815 they had suffered through The Year Without A Summer. Mount Tambora, a volcano in Indonesia had erupted and had severely disrupted Europe's climate, creating thick-clouds, relentless storms, and heavy snow throughout the summer. Crops failed, causing extensive famine across the country, especially among poor communities. This left Mohr's congregation impoverished, starving, and feeling hopeless. So Mohr set out to write a six-verse poem to show them that God still cared for them, and to help them feel hope for the future.

The following year, after moving to a new parish just south of Salzburg, Mohr sought the help of his friend, Franz Xaver Gruber, a teacher and musician, to compose music for his poem. They performed *Silent Night* for the first time a year later, on Christmas Eve in 1818, at their church, with Mohr playing his guitar.

The majority of Mohr's congregation worked along the Salzach River. Some were boat-builders, some had jobs shipping salt, and others just worked along the river. The river and the flowing water was a fundamental part of their life. To reflect this, Gruber composed the music for *Silent Night* in an Italian style known as siciliana. Originating in Sicily, the siciliana style was designed to mimic the sound of water and rolling waves. The next time you listen to *Silent Night*, do so picturing gentle waves lapping a shore and you'll see how effective Gruber's music is at evoking the feeling of water. The song breathes with the river.

The lyrics of *Silent Night* paint a portrait of the nativity scene, with Jesus as a new-born babe, lying in his manger in the first verse. The second verse introduces the shepherds quaking at the sight of a chorus of angels singing 'Hallelujah!', which juxtaposes the very nature of this being a silent night. The third verse focuses on Christ's purpose on Earth as a saviour, and marks the dawn of human redemption through God's grace.

Gruber's music has another beautiful effect in the hymn. Not only was it used to connect the church congregation to the Nativity story and make it relevant to them through the pattern of water in the siciliana style, but it also reflects Jesus's own words from John 7:37-39, which says:

> ...Jesus stood up and cried out, "If anyone thirsts, let him come to me and drink. Whoever believes in me, as the Scripture has said, 'Out of his heart will flow rivers of living water.'"

Through Gruber's use of the siciliana style, he ensured that the living water flowed through *Silent Night*. The feeling of gentle waves imbued in *Silent Night* not only represents the flow of the Salzach River but also embodies the very nature of the Holy Spirit.

Heavenly hosts sing, Hallelujah!

Henry Francis Lyte

Abide With Me

1847

Words

Henry Francis Lyte

Music

William H. Monk

Abide with me! fast falls the eventide;
The darkness deepens; Lord, with me abide!
When other helpers fail, and comforts flee,
Help of the helpless, O abide with me!

Swift to its close ebbs out life's little day;
Earth's joys grow dim, its glories pass away;
Change and decay in all around I see.
O Thou who changes not, abide with me!

Not a brief glance I beg, a passing word,
But as Thou dwell'st with Thy disciples, Lord,
Familiar, condescending, patient, free,
Come, not to sojourn, but abide with me.

Come not in terrors as the King of kings,
But kind and good, with healing on Thy wings;
Tears for all woes, a heart for every plea;
O Friend of sinners, thus abide with me!

Thou on my head in early youth didst smile,
And, though rebellious and perverse meanwhile,
Thou hast not left me, oft as I left Thee:
On to the close, O Lord, abide with me!

I need Thy presence every passing hour:
What but thy grace can foil the tempter's power?
Who like Thyself my guide and stay can be?
Through cloud and sunshine, O abide with me!

I fear no foe, with Thee at hand to bless:
Ills have no weight, and tears no bitterness.
Where is death's sting? where, grave, thy victory?
I triumph still, if Thou abide with me!

Hold Thou Thy Cross before my closing eyes,
Shine through the gloom, and point me to the skies:
Heaven's morning breaks, and earth's vain shadows flee;
In life, in death, O Lord, abide with me!

So they drew near to the village to which they were going. He acted as if he were going farther, but they urged him strongly, saying, "Stay with us, for it is toward evening and the day is now far spent." So he went in to stay with them. When he was at table with them, he took the bread and blessed and broke it and gave it to them. And their eyes were opened, and they recognized him. And he vanished from their sight.

Luke 24:28-31

Henry Francis Lyte was born in Scotland in 1793 and later studied at Trinity College in Dublin. He had originally intended to study medicine but made the decision to study Theology instead. Whilst at Trinity College he won three prizes for his poetry. His love of poetry and his deep knowledge of theology formed the foundation of his hymn writing. He published a huge quantity of hymns in his life, many of them were published in his two most famous collections: *Poems Chiefly Religious* (1833) and *The Spirit of the Psalms* (1834). *Abide With Me*, however, wasn't published in either of these collections. It wasn't published until after his death in 1847.

Despite being published posthumously, the inspiration for the hymn came when Henry Lyte was 27 years old. Lyte went to visit his dying friend, William Augustus Le Hunte, in County Wexford, in south-eastern Ireland. As Lyte sat with Le Hunte, Le Hunte repeated the phrase, *"Abide with me..."* over and over again. After leaving his friend's bedside, Lyte was so affected by his dying friends words, that he wrote verses around them and penned the first version of this hymn.

Twenty-seven years later, when Lyte was 54, he became terribly ill with tuberculosis. Both he and his family were aware that he was going to die soon. Every moment became special to his family, as they knew that each passing day was one day closer to his death. Remembering the words his friend had repeated 27 years earlier, Lyte rewrote his hymn, *Abide With Me*.

One of Lyte's final wishes was to deliver another sermon at the church he was serving at, in Lower Brixham, Devon. His family were surprised and alarmed at his request, and urged him to rethink his decision. Lyte said, *"It was better to wear out than to rust out,"* and, against his family's wishes, he delivered his final sermon to his congregation. They held on to his every word. After he delivered the sermon he gave his hymn, along with music that he had composed for it, to his daughter, Anna Hogg.

A few weeks later, Lyte travelled to Italy, where he was spending a lot of his time in the warmer climate. He died in Nice, which was then in the Kingdom of Sardinia. *Abide With Me* was sung for the very first time at Lyte's funeral.

Abide With Me was inspired by Luke 24. After Jesus' resurrection he appeared to his disciples on their way to the village of Emmaus but his disciples didn't recognise him. Jesus spoke to them about how necessary it was for the Christ to suffer and die. As they neared Emmaus, the disciples asked Jesus to stay with them, for it was almost the evening.

Lyte took this verse (Luke 24:29) and turned it into a metaphor for the brevity of human life. He altered the words from 'Abide with us' to 'Abide with me', making it all the more meaningful and deeply personal to those who sing it. The hymn is full of poetic metaphors for death, and the self-realisation of ones own death, which has made it a favourite hymn for funerals.

Throughout the hymn, Lyte asks God to abide with him. The hymn opens with those words, and each verse ends with those words. It's a beautiful, sorrowful prayer to God. Like the disciples, Lyte realised that a fleeting moment in Jesus' presence wasn't enough. The disciples asked Jesus to stay with them for a while longer, and Jesus obliged them. In the final line of the hymn, Lyte writes, *"In life, in death, O Lord, abide with me!"* Lyte wanted to be in God's presence until his final breath but knew that a lifetime with God wasn't enough, so he asked God to also abide with him in death.

And he said to him, "Truly, I say to you, today you will be with me in paradise." Luke 23:43

George J. Elvey

Crown Him With Many Crowns

1851

Words

Matthew Bridges

Music

George J. Elvey

Crown Him with many crowns,
The Lamb upon His throne;
Hark! how the heavenly
    anthem drowns
All music but its own!
Awake, my soul, and sing
Of Him Who died for thee;
And hail Him as thy matchless King
Through all eternity.

Crown Him the Virgin's Son!
The God incarnate born,
Whose arm those crimson
    trophies won
Which now His brow adorn,
Fruit of the Mystic Rose,
True Branch of Jesse's stem,
The Root whence mercy ever flows,
The Babe of Bethlehem!

Crown Him the Lord of Love!
Behold His hands and side,--
Those wounds, yet visible above,
In beauty glorified:
No angel in the sky
Can fully bear that sight,
But downward bends his
    wondering eye
At mysteries so bright.

Crown Him the Lord of Peace!
whose power a sceptre sways
In heaven and earth, that wars
    may cease,
And all be prayer and praise.
His reign shall know no end;
And round His piercèd feet
Fair flowers of Paradise extend
Their fragrance ever sweet.

Crown him the Lord of years!
  The Potentate of time,--
Creator of the rolling spheres,
  Ineffably sublime!
Glassed in a sea of light,
  Where everlasting waves
Reflect his throne,--the Infinite!
  Who lives,--and loves--and saves.

Crown Him the Lord of Heaven!
One with the Father known,--
And the blest Spirit, through
  Him given
From yonder Triune throne!
All hail, Redeemer, hail!
For Thou hast died for me:
thy praise and glory shall not fail
Throughout eternity.

His eyes are like a flame of fire, and on his head are many diadems, and he has a name written that no one knows but himself.

Revelation 19:12

Matthew Bridges was born in Essex, England, in 1800. He grew up in the Church of England because his father, the Rev Charles Bridges, was a priest of the Church of England. After being inspired by the theologian and poet John Henry Newman, Bridges later converted to Roman Catholicism at the age of 48, despite being openly sceptical of it at a young age. He remained a Roman Catholic until his death in 1894.

His life as a writer began at the age of 25, when he published his poem, *Jerusalem Regained*. He later published the book *The Roman Empire Under Constantine the Great*.

Bridges wrote *Crown Him With Many Crowns* when he was 51. He wanted to write original hymns, in the tradition of the Protestant church he grew up in, that shared his new Catholic ideologies. He later published two small hymnals, *Hymns of the Heart*, and *The Passion of Jesus*, that contained some of the new hymns he had written.

After *Crown Him With Many Crowns* found great popularity in churches across Britain, Godfrey Thring, an Anglican priest, was worried that Protestant Churches were now singing an overtly Catholic hymn. To balance out the Catholic theology, he decided to write an additional six verses for the hymn. Their verses are now often intertwined, with churches choosing which verses they want to sing.

Crown Him With Many Crowns was inspired by Revelation 19:12, in which a vision of Jesus riding a white horse is seen to be wearing many crowns (or diadems in the ESV translation). The many crowns that Christ wears, cements him as the complete Lord of creation.

Each verse of the hymn begins with the crowning of Jesus as a new title, celebrating the many aspects of who he is: Jesus is the Virgin's Son, the Lord of Love, the Lord of Peace, the Lord of Years, the Lord of Heaven. Thring also continued this repetition in his additional verses, which also crowned Jesus as the Son of God, the Lord of Light, the Lord of Life, and the Lord of lords.

Crown Him With Many Crowns is a jubilant celebration of who our Saviour is. It offers us a chance to reflect on Jesus' character, and his titles and triumphantly proclaim who he is to us personally.

Awake, my soul, and sing

Joseph Medlicott Scriven

What A Friend We Have In Jesus

1855

Words

Joseph Medlicott Scriven

Music

Charles C. Converse

What a friend we have in Jesus,
All our sins and griefs to bear;
What a privilege to carry
Every thing to God in prayer.
Oh, what peace we often forfeit,
Oh, what needless pain we bear;—
All because we do not carry
Every thing to God in prayer.

Have we trials and temptations?
Is there trouble anywhere?
We should never be discouraged,
Take it to the Lord in prayer.
Can we find a friend so faithful,
Who will all our sorrows share;
Jesus knows our every weakness,
Take it to the Lord in prayer.

Are we weak and heavy laden,
Cumbered with a load of care;
Precious Saviour, still our refuge,
Take it to the Lord in prayer.
Do thy friends despise, forsake thee,
Take it to the Lord in prayer;
In his arms he'll take and shield thee,
Thou wilt find a solace there.

"Come to me, all who labour and are heavy laden,
and I will give you rest."

Matthew 11:28

Joseph Scriven faced more trials and heartbreak than many others. He was born in 1819 in Banbridge, Ireland and went on to earn his degree at Trinity College, Dublin. He aspired to a career in the military, and signed up for a military college, but his ambitions were dashed because of an illness.

In 1844, following his illness, he planned to settle down and marry his fiancée. Unfortunately, the night before their wedding his bride-to-be had a terrible accident and drowned. He was only 25.

After her death he moved to Ontario, Canada, to begin his new life. There he fell in love again, and was engaged to be married to a woman named Eliza Rice. Unfortunately tragedy was to strike twice as Eliza caught Pneumonia and died only two weeks before their wedding.

Scriven, heartbroken, found himself without a reliable income and was dependent on his friends and family for accommodation. He then decided to live his life according to the Sermon on the Mount as literally as possible. He lived a life of poverty and devoted his time to helping others. He gave as much as he could, and shared what little he had. For ten years he helped the poor and the handicapped as much as he could, and in any way that they needed. He made himself available to them day and night, and found a new purpose in serving others.

Scriven received news that his mother, who was still living in Ireland, had become very ill and didn't have long left to live. Since he was living in Canada, and had limited funds, he couldn't afford to travel to Ireland to see her before she passed.

Because he wasn't able to see her, he decided to write her a poem instead, which he hoped would comfort her. The poem he wrote would later be set to music and become *What A Friend We Have In Jesus*.

Reading Scriven's words again, after knowing the pain he must have felt, makes it all the more personal. When he writes, *'What a friend we have in Jesus, All our sins and griefs to bear'* we know the weight of the griefs that he was bearing. The weight must have been unbearable. And for Jesus to bear that grief for him… well, only a friend could do that.

He then goes on to say, *'What a privilege to carry, Everything to God in prayer.'* Scriven knew the importance of prayer, and offering his grief to God. We can only imagine the long, personal, heartfelt prayers that Scriven must have prayed in his grief. It would have been like a late night conversation between friends, where one friend is opening up their heart, and the other friend is lovingly listening.

He not only knew the importance of prayer, but he saw it as his privilege. It's a privilege that God has offered to everyone but it's a privilege that not everyone accepts. We can see this in the second half of the first verse, where Scriven writes:

> *Oh, what peace we often forfeit,*
> *Oh, what needless pain we bear;—*
> *All because we do not carry*
> *Every thing to God in prayer.*

From this, we get a small glimpse into what Scriven's grief may have been like. After the death of his first fiancée, he may have held onto that grief as tightly as he could, and felt every inch of pain that came with it. But then he prayed to God, and asked Him to bear his grief for him, and God accepted. He would have felt a rush of peace filling the void where his grief once lay. Grief is like a heavy rock that kills the grass beneath it but once the rock is lifted the grass can grow again.

The final three lines of the hymn are a tender description of Scriven's relationship with God, and paints such a gentle portrait of the loving, protective nature of God:

Take it to the Lord in prayer;
In his arms he'll take and shield thee,
Thou wilt find a solace there.

**What a privilege
to carry,
Every thing to God
in prayer**

Anna Bartlett Warner

Jesus Loves Me, This I Know

1859

Words

Anna Bartlett Warner

Music

William B. Bradbury

Jesus loves me! this I know,
For the Bible tells me so;
Little ones to him belong;
They are weak, but he is strong.

Yes, Jesus loves me;
Yes, Jesus loves me;
Yes, Jesus loves me;
The Bible tells me so.

Jesus loves me! he who died,
Heaven's gate to open wide;
He will wash away my sin,
Let his little child come in.

Jesus loves me! he will stay
Close beside me all the way;
If I love him when I die.
He will take me home on high.

"As the Father has loved me, so have I loved you. Abide in my love"

John 15:9

In 1943, during the second world war, John F. Kennedy was the lieutenant of a patrol torpedo boat near the Solomon Islands. It was part of the Solomon Islands Campaign, which was a counteroffensive initiative to defend communication and supply lines in the South Pacific. Kennedy's boat, the PT-109, was rammed by a Japanese destroyer. They had been idling on one engine to avoid detection, but in turn failed to detect the approaching Japanese ship, which was sailing without lights and was steering towards them.

After spotting the Japanese destroyer they had less than 10 seconds to act. The destroyer collided with Kennedy's ship, cutting in two, and caused a 100-foot-high fireball to erupt into the air.

Kennedy was able to rescue several of his crew members who were severely burned. For such a disaster it was a miracle that so few people were injured. It was Kennedy's act of bravery that made him a war hero and that in part led to him being elected as president in 1961.

Two Solomon Islanders, Biuku Gasa and Eroni Kumana, spotted the explosion and went out in their canoe to find survivors. They rescued Kennedy and his men and took them to safety.

Although they struggled to communicate with each other, the crew of the PT-109 and their rescuers shared together in singing *Jesus Loves Me, This I Know*. Gasa and Kumana had learned the song from Seventh-day Adventist missionaries who had come to their island.

Anna Bartlett Warner, born in Long Island, New York, in 1827, was an American writer. She wrote 31 novels of her own, often using the pseudonym Amy Lothrop, and wrote several books with her sister Susan Warner.

Jesus Loves Me, This I Know, is probably her most famous work. It was originally written as a poem for the novel *Say and Seal*, which she wrote with her sister. In the novel, a young, dying boy asks his Sunday school teacher to sing him a song. The teacher chooses to sing *Jesus Loves Me*. In the book, a fourth verse is also sung, which goes:

> *Jesus loves me—loves me still,*
> *Though I'm very weak and ill;*
> *From his shining throne on high,*
> *Comes to watch me where I lie.*

The second line of the fourth verse, *'Though I'm very weak and ill,'* was relevant to the story but not to the hymn in a church context so the fourth verse has since been omitted from the hymn.

The original poem didn't include the refrain, *'Yes, Jesus loves me...'*. This was added by the hymn's composer, William Bradbury, in 1862, when he published the hymn in a collection of Sunday school songs called *Bradbury's Golden Chain And Shower For The Sabbath School*. It then went on to become one of the most popular children's hymns worldwide.

Jesus Loves Me, This I Know, is a simple song, with a clean memorable melody, and a theology so pure you could drink it. It was able to cross cultural boundaries and bring people together in the middle of war. It doesn't matter if it was intended to be sung by children or adults. What matters is that it is a reminder that Jesus loves us and a shared faith in God unifies us.

In 1 Corinthians 1:10, Paul wrote to the church in Corinth and told them:

> *I appeal to you, brothers, by the name of our Lord Jesus Christ, that all of you agree, and that there be no divisions among you, but that you be united in the same mind and the same judgment.*

Yes,
Jesus loves me

Charitie Lees Bancroft

Before The Throne Of God Above

1863

Words

Charitie Lees Bancroft

Music

Vikki Cook

Before the throne of God above
I have a strong, a perfect plea;
a great high priest, whose name
  is Love,
who ever lives and pleads for me.

My name is written on his hands,
my name is hidden in his heart;
I know that while in heaven he stands
no tongue can force me to depart.

When Satan tempts me to despair
and tells me of the guilt within,
upward I look, and see him there
who made an end of all my sin.

Because the sinless Saviour died,
my sinful soul is counted free;
for God the just is satisfied
to look on him and pardon me.

Behold him there! the risen Lamb,
my perfect, spotless Righteousness,
the great unchangeable I AM,
the King of glory and of grace!

One with my Lord, I cannot die:
my soul is purchased by his blood,
my life is safe with Christ on high,
with Christ my saviour and my God.

My little children, I am writing these things to you so that you may not sin. But if anyone does sin, we have an advocate with the Father, Jesus Christ the righteous.

1 John 2:1

Charitie Lees Bancroft was born in Dublin, Ireland in 1841. She was the fourth child of Rev. Dr. George Sidney Smith, a minister of the parish of Aghalurcher, where it is likely that Bancroft wrote *Before The Throne Of God Above*.

Initially she had titled the hymn *The Advocate*. In her eyes, Jesus was her advocate. He supported her and commended her before God, and even went as far as to die, to purchase her soul with his blood, so that God would *'look on him and pardon me'*.

Bancroft presents us with a beautiful and personal explanation of the crucifixion. The result of Christ's death is that he can stand before God as our advocate. He stands before the throne of God and pleas for us. And because the sinless Saviour died, our sinful souls are counted free.

The hymn gained great popularity in the 1870's, and was even published in Charles Spurgeon's *Our Own Hymn Book* fourteen years later. But then the hymn's popularity waned and almost disappeared for a hundred years until the 1970's when the hymn began reappearing in hymnals and gradually grew in popularity.

It wasn't until 1997 that *Before The Throne* had its second revival, the revival that cemented this hymn as a Sunday service staple.

Vikki Cook, of Sovereign Church, Florida, wrote her own arrangement for the hymn. It is Cook's arrangement and melody that you are most likely familiar with. Before then, the hymn was often paired with traditional hymn tunes, most notably *Sweet Hour Of Prayer*, composed by William Batchelder Bradbury in 1861, and even *Jerusalem*, by C. Hubert H. Parry in 1916.

Vikki Cook resonated with the words so much that she was compelled to compose her own arrangement of the hymn, and refresh it for a new generation of churchgoers. Through her new melody she was able to help people connect with God and understand the beautiful, powerful and personal nature of having a saviour in Jesus.

I would just like to add a personal note here. Cook has achieved what I am striving for with *Hymns of Note*. She has taken the words to an old hymn and has shown the world just how relevant they still are. Bancroft's line, *'the great unchangeable I AM,'* cements this notion that true words written about God hold their truth and significance as much now as they did when they were written, no matter how long ago that was.

Philip Paul Bliss

Man Of Sorrows

Words

Philip Paul Bliss

Music

Philip Paul Bliss

"Man of Sorrows," what a name
For the Son of God, who came
Ruined sinners to reclaim:
Hallelujah! what a Saviour!

Bearing shame and scoffing rude,
In my place condemned He stood,
Sealed my pardon with His blood:
Hallelujah! what a Saviour!

Guilty, vile and helpless we;
Spotless Lamb of God was He;
"Full atonement!" can it be?
Hallelujah! what a Saviour!

Lifted up was He to die;
"It is finished," was His cry;
Now in heaven exalted high,
Hallelujah! what a Saviour!

When he comes, our glorious King,
All His ransomed home to bring,
Then anew this song we'll sing,
Hallelujah! what a Saviour!

He was despised and rejected by men,
a man of sorrows and acquainted with grief;
and as one from whom men hide their faces
he was despised, and we esteemed him not.

Isaiah 53:3

Phillip P. Bliss was one of the most significant American gospel musicians of his time. He was born in a log cabin in Pennsylvania in 1838. Both he and his sister, Mary Wilson, developed a love of music from a young age. Mary went on to become a gospel singer, and Bliss went on to write around 240 hymns. He wrote his first when he was twenty-six and wrote his last when he was just thirty-eight. He even composed music for other writers, one of his most notable being the music for *It Is Well With My Soul*, written by Horatio Spafford.

His life was tragically cut short in 1876, when he was travelling with his wife by train. As they were crossing a bridge near Ashtabula, Ohio, the bridge collapsed and sent the train crashing down into the ravine below.

Man Of Sorrows tells the story of Christ's death, resurrection, and second coming, from our perspective as sinful people. Verse one starts by calling Jesus the *'Man of Sorrows'*, foreshadowing the amount of pain and suffering he was going to endure. It is taken straight out of Isaiah 53. The first verse also lays out Christ's mission: he came to reclaim ruined sinners.

The second verse references how Jesus was mocked after his trial and before his crucifixion, and shows how the suffering he endured was meant for us. He was standing in our place.

The third verse juxtaposes Christ as a spotless, sinless lamb with us as guilty, vile and helpless sinners. The fourth verse shows Christ's death, and his famous words, *"It is finished"* before being exalted in heaven. And the fifth, and final, verse announces Christ's second coming.

At the end of each verse is the repeated line: *'Hallelujah! What a saviour!'*, which is also this hymn's alternate title. The repetition of the final line reminds us of Christ's suffering, death, and resurrection, that he deserves to be praised, and that everything he had done was part of his mission to reclaim ruined sinners.

The word *'Hallelujah'* is the same in almost every language. It is a jubilant exclamation that praises God. The angels sing it in heaven, as mentioned in Revelation 19, and we sing it on Earth. The fact that *'Hallelujah'* is the same in almost all languages emphasises our unity through Christ, no matter who we are or what language we speak. We are all the ruined sinners that Christ came to reclaim, and because of that we can all rejoice in God together.

Edmond Louis Budry

Thine Is The Glory

1904

Words

Edmond Louis Budry

Translation

Richard Birch Hoyle

Music

George Frederick Handel

Thine is the glory, risen, conqu'ring Son;
Endless is the victory, Thou o'er death hast won;
Angels in bright raiment rolled the stone away,
Kept the folded grave clothes where Thy body lay.

Thine is the glory, risen conqu'ring Son,
Endless is the vict'ry, Thou o'er death hast won.

Lo! Jesus meets us, risen from the tomb;
Lovingly He greets us, scatters fear and gloom;
Let the church with gladness, hymns of triumph sing;
For her Lord now liveth, death hath lost its sting.

No more we doubt Thee, glorious Prince of life;
Life is naught without Thee; aid us in our strife;
Make us more than conqu'rors, through Thy deathless love:
Bring us safe through Jordan to Thy home above.

"O death, where is your victory?
O death, where is your sting?"

1 Corinthians 15:55

Edmond Budry was a hymnist and translator from Vevey, Switzerland. He studied theology in Lausanne before becoming a pastor in 1881. As well as writing his own hymns, he also translated hymns written in German, English, and Latin into his native French. More often than not, Budry would translate the hymns into his own words, rewriting them, and improving them.

The original title of *Thine Is The Glory* was *A Toi la gloire, ô Ressuscité*, which translates to '*Glory to you, O Risen One*'.

Thine Is The Glory, also known as *Thine Be The Glory*, is a celebration of Christ's resurrection. Budry purposefully wrote the hymn to the tune of Judas Maccabeus by Handel, which has a strong military feel to it. He did this to emphasise the power of Christ's resurrection, because Jesus didn't just come back to life, he conquered death. His crucifixion and resurrection was a war on sin, and it was a war that he won.

The first verse of *Thine Is The Glory* starts by revealing the power of the resurrection. It shows Jesus as a victorious conqueror and then recounts the moment that the angels rolled away the heavy stone that had been placed in front of his tomb, to prevent his followers from stealing his body.

The second verse speaks of the relief that Jesus' followers feel after learning of the resurrection. His victory scatters fear and gloom. There would have been a fear that Jesus' death meant that he wasn't God, after all. But Jesus' resurrection proved him to be who he claimed to be. Budry then addresses us, the modern church, directly. He calls for us to be glad and to sing hymns triumphantly, because Jesus is alive and, to quote 1 Corinthians 15:55, death has lost its sting. This line in particular would have held a personal importance to Budry. Not long before writing this hymn, his wife had passed away. He knew that even though he could mourn his wife's earthly death, she was now alive in Christ. And holding that knowledge in your heart really cuts away the sting of death.

In the third verse, in the original French, Budry crowns Jesus as the Prince of peace but Richard Hoyle changed this in his translation to Prince of life. He did this to further emphasise Christ's victory over death.

Thine Is The Glory is a firm Easter favourite and is often included in the British royal family's Easter services because of its joyous exploration of the resurrection and what it means for us, as Christians.

Sung between each verse is a refrain, which emphasises this even further. It pulls directly from 1 Corinthians 15:57, where Paul writes:

> *But thanks be to God, who gives us the victory through our Lord Jesus Christ.*

So as we sing this hymn, we know that Christ has emerged victorious from his empty tomb and that death has been conquered.

Charles Albert Tindley

Nothing Between My Soul And The Saviour

1905

Words

Charles Albert Tindley

Music

Charles Albert Tindley

Nothing between my soul and the Saviour,
Naught of this world's delusive dream;
I have renounced all sinful pleasure,
Jesus is mine; there's nothing between.

Nothing between my soul and the Saviour,
So that His blessed face may be seen;
Nothing preventing the least of His favor,
Keep the way clear! let nothing between.

Nothing between, like worldly pleasure,
Habits of life, though harmless they seem,
Must not my heart from Him ever sever,
He is my all, there's nothing between.

Nothing between, like pride or station;
Self or friends shall not intervene,
Though it may cost me much tribulation,
I am resolved; there's nothing between.

Nothing between, e'en many hard trials,
Though the whole world against me convene;
Watching with pray'r and much self-denial,
I'll triumph at last, with nothing between.

Do not love the world or the things in the world. If anyone loves the world, the love of the Father is not in him. For all that is in the world—the desires of the flesh and the desires of the eyes and pride of life—is not from the Father but is from the world. And the world is passing away along with its desires, but whoever does the will of God abides forever.

1 John 2:15-17

Charles Albert Tindley was known as the father of African American Hymnody and the originator of African American gospel music. He was born in Berlin, Maryland, in 1851. His father was a slave but his mother was a free woman. When Charles was two years old his mother passed away. In order to ensure his freedom from slavery, Charles was adopted by his mother's sister, who was also a free woman. If he had stayed to live with his father he probably would have lost his status as a free man and would have been forced into slavery.

When Charles was old enough, his father hired him out to work. Charles found himself working amongst slaves, without being a slave himself. It was quite common at the time for free men to be hired out and work on plantations. Despite being free, Charles would have experienced the reality of slavery, the main difference being that Charles would have been paid for his work and, at the end of the day, he was allowed to go home.

After the American Civil War ended in 1865, Charles moved to Philadelphia with his wife and committed himself to a life of learning. He vowed to, *"...learn at least one new thing—a thing I did not know the day before—each day."*

In 1902 he became the pastor at Bainbridge St. Methodist Episcopal Church, where he had taken an unpaid position as a sexton – or janitor – a few years earlier. As the pastor of the church the congregation grew rapidly. In 1916 he published his hymnal *New Songs Of Paradise!*. The book became so successful that people flocked to Charles' church to hear him preach. There was such an influx of new members that they had to buy a new church building. By 1924 his church had a membership of over 7,000 people. The leadership was a representation of the community, with African Americans, white Americans, Italians, Germans, Mexicans, and a host of others. No matter what someone's background was, if they went to Charles' church it was more than likely that they were represented in the leadership.

Charles Tindley wrote *Nothing Between My Soul And The Saviour* in 1905. He wrote whilst he was in the process of negotiating the purchase of a new church for his growing congregation. It was an emotional time for him, mixed with stress, joy, and disappointment. Whilst working on a sermon one day, a gust of wind blew through an open window and lifted the papers from his table as he was working. Some of the papers landed on top of the sermon he was writing, forcing him to stop. As the paper covered his sermon, Charles thought to himself, *"Now, now, let nothing between,"* and the idea for the hymn was born.

The main theme of the hymn is that we shouldn't let anything come between Jesus and us. Charles highlights several examples throughout the hymn. In the first verse he mentions the world's delusive dream. He's talking about how the attractive things of the world are deceptive and fleeting, like a dream. Charles then says that he has renounced all sinful pleasure, not letting the world come between him and Jesus.

The second verse refers to habits of life. Charles is warning against becoming so stuck in our ways, and so fixated on living our life a certain habitual way, that we don't leave any room for Jesus. Instead of worshiping God, we're worshiping the life we've made for ourselves.

In the third verse he talks about pride and station. He could be referring to the division between white Americans and African Americans. Pro-slavery white Americans prided themselves on the pureness of their race and their status above others. Undoubtedly, this stood between them and God. In 1 John 4:20 Jesus says:

> *"If anyone says, "I love God," and hates his brother, he is a liar; for he who does not love his brother whom he has seen cannot love God whom he has not seen."*

In the final verse, Charles talks about the many hard trials that he has had to face. There are many hymns that were written after facing a tragedy or as a result of suffering and they are testaments to how the hymn writers kept their eyes and focus on God during those times. Living as an African American during the American Civil War would have been filled with trials, suffering, and hardship, and yet, through it all, Charles knew that he couldn't let any of them stand between his soul and his Saviour.

Frederick M. Lehman

The Love Of God

1917

Words

Frederick M. Lehman

Music

Frederick M. Lehman

The love of God is greater far
Than tongue or pen can ever tell;
It goes beyond the highest star,
And reaches to the lowest hell;
The guilty pair, bowed down
   with care,
God gave His Son to win;
His erring child He reconciled,
And pardoned from his sin.

O love of God, how rich and pure!
How measureless and strong!
It shall forevermore endure
The saints' and angels' song.

When years of time shall pass away,
And earthly thrones and kingdoms fall,
When men, who here refuse to pray,
On rocks and hills and mountains call,
God's love so sure, shall still endure,
All measureless and strong;
Redeeming grace to Adam's race—
The saints' and angels' song.

Could we with ink the ocean fill,
And were the skies of
   parchment made,
Were every stalk on earth a quill,
And every man a scribe by trade,
To write the love of God above,
Would drain the ocean dry.
Nor could the scroll contain the whole,
Though stretched from sky to sky.

So we have come to know and to believe the love that God has for us. God is love, and whoever abides in love abides in God, and God abides in him.

1 John 4:16

Frederick Lehman emigrated from Germany when he was four years old. He and his family settled in Iowa. A few years later, when he was eleven years old, he decided to become a Christian. Since dedicating his life to Christ he started to write poetry and then, when he became the pastor of a church in Audubon, Iowa, he took up writing hymns too. Over the course of his life he wrote hundreds of hymns and published five hymnals.

Lehman later relocated to Pasadena, California, in 1917. After losing a lot of money in a failed business endeavour, Lehman took a job at a packing house, where he would pack oranges and lemons into wooden boxes.

One Sunday evening he heard a sermon about the love of God. He was so moved by it that he couldn't get it out of his head. He could hardly sleep that night. He found himself tossing and turning in bed, overwhelmed with the love of God, and celebrating his salvation. The following day, as he was driving to work, he started forming his thoughts into a song. The song occupied his thoughts as he packed away the oranges and lemons. He just couldn't wait to write them down. He found himself unable to concentrate on work, so he found a scrap of paper and a pencil stub and pushed a lemon box against the wall to sit on, as he jotted down the first two verses.

He rushed home from work, and went straight to his piano. He began arranging his words, and tapping out a melody until both words and music came together in harmony. He had written the first two verses and composed the melody for them but he had reached a stand still. At the time, hymns needed at least three verses, otherwise they weren't deemed to be complete. He struggled to write a third verse, the first two came so easily, but he just couldn't write a third verse that he thought was worthy of his song.

Whilst preparing to move to California, Lehman had heard an evangelist talk about a poem that had been found scribbled onto the wall of an inmate's room in a prison. No one knew who the convict was, or why he had been imprisoned. Lehman was fascinated with the poem and he wrote it down on a piece of paper that he later used a bookmark. Apparently, after the inmate's death, one of the men hired to repaint the cell was so impressed with the poem that he wrote it down and shared it with his pastor.

The poem was this:

> Could we with ink the ocean fill,
> And were the skies of parchment made,
> Were every stalk on earth a quill,
> And every man a scribe by trade,
> To write the love of God above,
> Would drain the ocean dry.
> Nor could the scroll contain the whole,
> Though stretched from sky to sky.

As Lehman was sat at his piano, he remembered this poem. He hunted for the book that it was kept in and when he found it he sat down at his piano. This was the moment that it all came to gather. He gently played the melody and sang the poem over the music. The melody and the words of the poem fit together perfectly. It was a miracle. You can almost imagine the astonished smile on Lehman's face as he rejoiced.

The poem is now recognised to have been written almost a thousand years earlier by a Jewish rabbi called Meir ben Isaac Nehorai, known as Rabbi Meir of Worms. It was a single stanza in an epic acrostic poem called Hadamut. The poem was originally written in Hebrew, and it is assumed that the prisoner himself had translated this verse into English, and, amazingly, into the exact same metre that Lehman used for his most famous hymn.

The words of the poem seem to be inspired by a verse from the Qur'an that reads:

> *If all the trees on earth were pens,*
> *and the ocean were ink,*
> *replenished by seven more oceans,*
> *the writing of God's wonderful signs and creations*
> *would not be exhausted;*
> *surely God is All-Mighty, All-Wise.*

The hymn is all about how vast, and how immeasurable, God's love is for us. No one could ever express it completely. The universe itself could not contain it. It would reach higher than the stars, and lower than the depths of hell. No amount of time, and no amount of sinners, could ever outweigh the love of God.

The Love of God was written by four people from at least three different religions: the original inspiration of Islam's Qur'an, the Hebrew poem written by a Jewish Rabbi, the English translation provided by the unnamed prisoner, and the final composition by Frederick Lehman, a Christian man who knew how boundless and timeless God's love is.

112

The story and history behind this hymn really is a testament to the words contained within it:

The love of God is greater far
Than tongue or pen can ever tell.

Thomas O. Chisholm

Great Is Thy Faithfulness

1923

Words

Thomas O. Chisholm

Music

William Marion Runyan

"Great is Thy faithfulness", O God my Father,
There is no shadow of turning with Thee;
Thou changest not, Thy compassions, they fail not;
As Thou hast been Thou forever wilt be.

"Great is Thy faithfulness!
Great is Thy faithfulness!"
Morning by morning new mercies I see;
All I have needed Thy hand hath provided;--
"Great is Thy faithfulness,"
Lord, unto me!

Summer and winter, and springtime and harvest,
Sun, moon and stars in their courses above,
Join with all nature in manifold witness
To Thy great faithfulness, mercy and love.

Pardon for sin and a peace that endureth,
Thy own dear presence to cheer and to guide;
Strength for today and bright hope for tomorrow,
Blessings all mine, with ten thousand beside!

The steadfast love of the Lord never ceases;
his mercies never come to an end;
they are new every morning;
great is your faithfulness.

Lamentations 3:22-23

Thomas Obadiah Chisholm was born in a log cabin in Franklin, Kentucky, in 1866. Despite not having any formal education, he became a teacher when he was just 16. At the age of 27 he went to a revival led by Dr. Henry Clay Morrison, a Methodist Evangelist and president of Asbury College. It was at the revival that Chisholm became a Christian. He made the decision to become a minister and was ordained in 1903. He then served as a Methodist minister in Scottsville, Kentucky. His pastoral career lasted only a year, due to suffering from poor health.

Chisholm moved his family to Indiana, so he could recover his health, and then to New Jersey in 1916, where he took a job as an insurance salesman.

Chisholm loved to write poetry. Over the course of his life he had written over 1,200 poems, and had published 800 of them. In 1923 he sent a collection of his poetry to Rev. William H. Runyan, a musician and an editor of Hope Publishing Company, in Chicago.

When Runyan read *Great Is Thy Faithfulness*, he was astounded by its depth and complexity and decided to set it to music. Runyan wrote:

"This particular poem held such an appeal that I prayed most earnestly that my tune might carry over its message in a worthy way, and the subsequent history of its use indicates that God answered prayer."

In 1954, George Beverly Shea, a Canadian-born singer, introduced the hymn at Billy Graham's Crusades in the UK. It became so popular that it cemented its place as one of England's favourite hymns.

The three verses each reveal God's faithfulness in different ways.

The first verse conveys God's faithfulness in his Word, and his unchanging nature, as described in James 1:17:

Every good gift and every perfect gift is from above, coming down from the Father of lights, with whom there is no variation or shadow due to change.

The second verse expresses God's faithfulness in creation. Chisholm writes of the unification of creation, the seasons, the sun, the moon, and the stars, and the whole of nature, and how they all join together to declare God's faithfulness, mercy and love.

The third verse reveals God's faithfulness to us personally and connects God with humanity. The line, *'Pardon for sin and a peace that endureth,'* reflects the forgiveness of our sins, by God, because of Jesus, and beautifully states the peace that follows forgiveness.

By his own account, Chisholm was an ordinary man who lived a normal humdrum life. He described himself as *"just an old shoe."* But it is his ordinariness that makes this hymn so remarkable. It proves to show that God is faithful to everyone. He isn't only faithful to the adventurous, or to those who embark on missionary crusades, or to those who experience tremendous hardships in their lives. God is faithful to everyone. Even an old shoe, like Chisholm.

To finish, I'd like to share an excerpt from a letter that Chisholm wrote when he was 75 years old:

"My income has not been large at any time due to impaired health in the earlier years which has followed me on until now. Although I must not fail to record here the unfailing faithfulness of a covenant-keeping God and that He has given me many wonderful displays of His providing care, for which I am filled with astonishing gratefulness."

Morning
by morning
new mercies I see

How To Write A Hymn

There are two occasions when I feel like I'm most connected to God: when I'm in nature and when I'm singing worship songs.

Hymns are such an important part of worship. Even though there are thousands upon thousands of hymns that have been written, I want to encourage you to write your own.

You don't need to be musical, have a formal education, or be a writer to write a hymn. If you are thinking to yourself, *'I couldn't possibly write a hymn,'* or, *'this part of the book isn't for me'* allow me to tell you that this part of the book is definitely for you, and you absolutely can write a hymn. In fact, I'm challenging you right now to write your own hymn. What have you got to lose? You don't have to share it with anyone, it can just be between you and God. You don't even have to make it 'perfect', if such a thing is even possible.

Not only am I challenging you to write your own hymn but you have my permission to write an imperfect hymn. You might end up with a hymn that you think is poorly written but I think it's more likely that you'll end up with a hymn that you're proud of because you accomplished something new and got to worship God whilst you were doing it.

So now that you're feeling encouraged and are about to write your own hymn, where do you even start?

1. Choose A Topic

What's the theme of your hymn? What is it that you want to write about? In *Great Is Thy Faithfulness* Thomas O. Chisholm wanted to write about the faithfulness of God. In *While Shepherds Watched Their Flocks* Nahum Tate wanted to retell the story of the shepherds encountering the angels on the night Jesus was born. In *The Lord's My Shepherd* Francis Rous decided to adapt Psalm 23.

These are three viable options on how to choose a topic: choose a general theme, recount a biblical story, or versify a passage of scripture.

I'm going to write my own hymn alongside you, to show you how to do it. For my hymn I'm going to choose a general theme. As I write this, we're seeing what is hopefully the tail end of a pandemic. It has been a scary and uncertain time, so I want to write about fear and why we don't have to be afraid.

What topic have you chosen?

2. Back It Up With Scripture

Once you have chosen your topic, expand upon it with scripture. It's important that hymns are biblically accurate, that's why I've paired the lyrics of hymns in this book with scripture that backs them up. Not only does it help us to see how the hymnist was inspired, but it also shows us that what we are singing is truthful and biblically sound.

For my hymn, the theme of not being afraid appears hundreds of times in the Bible – it's something that is obviously important to God - so we have plenty of scripture we can look at for inspiration.

Before I write the first verse of my hymn I'm going to look for scripture that is relevant to the theme and that speaks to me on a personal level.

Okay, I've chosen the following verses for inspiration. I have also emboldened the relevant lines that I'm going to work into my hymn:

> **The Lord is on my side; I will not fear.**
> *What can man do to me?*
> (Psalm 118:6)

> *For you have been a stronghold to the poor,*
> *a stronghold to the needy in his distress,*
> **a shelter from the storm** *and a shade from the heat;*
> *for the breath of the ruthless is like a storm against a wall,*
> (Isaiah 25:4)

> *But now thus says the Lord,*
> *he who created you, O Jacob,*
> *he who formed you, O Israel:*
> **"Fear not, for I have redeemed you;**
> **I have called you by name, you are mine.**
> (Isaiah 43:1)

Now that I've found my inspiration I need to reword it and restructure it so that it takes the form of a verse.

Which verses have you chosen as inspiration for your hymn?

3. Choose A Metre

I'm not going to go deep into music theory, but it's important to talk about metres. What is a metre? A metre (or meter) is a structure that dictates the number of syllables in each line of a verse. It ensures that the number of syllables remains consistent, making it easier to pair with music.

Amazing Grace uses the Common Metre, which alternates between 8 syllables and 6 syllables over four lines. The first and third lines each have 8 syllables and the second and fourth lines each have 6 syllables. It would be written as 8.6.8.6 (or sometimes 86.86). You may have noticed these groups of numbers at the top of the pages in your hymn books, these are telling you what metre the hymn is in.

> *Amazing grace, how sweet the sound* (**8**)
> *that saved a wretch like me.* (**6**)
> *I once was lost, but now am found,* (**8**)
> *was blind, but now I see.* (**6**)

Another popular metre is the Long Metre, which is four lines of eight syllables each. It's written as 8.8.8.8. or 88.88. *When I Survey The Wondrous Cross* is written in this metre.

> *When I survey the wond'rous Cross* (**8**)
> *On which the Prince of Glory dy'd,* (**8**)
> *My richest Gain I count but Loss,* (**8**)
> *And pour Contempt on all my Pride.* (**8**)

There are many different metres you can use. When you start writing you might find that one comes naturally. Alternatively you might have a melody that you'd like to compose lyrics for. In that case, the metre will be dictated by the music.

At this point you should decide whether you want your hymn to rhyme or not. If you want your hymn to rhyme, you need to be consistent and choose a rhyme scheme that works for your hymn and stick with it.

For my hymn, I've decided to not make it rhyme and to use the Common Metre: 8.6.8.6.

4. Start Writing

Now that you've chosen your topic, backed it up with scripture, and have selected a metre, you can start writing your hymn.

For my hymn, I'm going to start by rewriting the scripture I've chosen to back up my theme so that it fits the metre.

The Lord is on my side; I will not fear. (Psalm 118:6)

'The Lord is on my side, I will not fear' is 10 syllables long. So I need to rearrange it and cut it down so that it's only 8 syllables long:

I will not fear, you're on my side.

That works!

...a shelter from the storm... (Isaiah 25:4)

"...a shelter from the storm" is 6 syllables, so that fits the Common Metre. However, I would like to reword it to make it more personal, so I will change it to *'My shelter...'*. I also prefer the wording in the King James Version: *'...a refuge from the storm'*.

I'll write it as:

> *My refuge from the storm.*

Perfect!

> *"Fear not, for I have redeemed you;*
> > *I have called you by name, you are mine.*
>
> (Isaiah 43:1)

The first line from Isaiah 43:1 fits the metre, but it's God speaking to us. I'd like to keep this song as a song of praise where we are singing it to God. I also like the wording from Psalm 118:6, *'I will not fear...'* so I'd like to keep that and maybe use it at the beginning of every other line. This way I can use the main theme of the hymn as a heartbeat throughout the song.

> *I will not fear, I am redeemed,*

I like the line *'I have called you by name'* from the same verse, so I'm going to finish off verse one by rewording it slightly:

> *You summoned me by name.*

And just like that, I've written the first verse of my hymn:

> *I will not fear, you're on my side,* (Psalm 118:6)
> *My refuge from the storm.* (Isaiah 25:4)
> *I will not fear, I am redeemed,* (Isaiah 43:1)
> *You summoned me by name.* (Isaiah 43:1)

Hopefully I'm demystifying the hymn-writing process, and showing you just how doable it actually is. Now I'm going to write a chorus for my hymn. Some hymns only have verses, whilst others might have a simple refrain, but I would like a separate four-line chorus to be sung between each verse.

For the chorus I want to change it up slightly. I'm going to keep the metre the same, although you could change it if you wanted to, but I want to deviate from the verses so that it stands out. I also want to end with a strong proclamation that defines the theme of the hymn. In Psalm 56:11, David writes, *'I shall not be afraid.'* I'll change *'shall'* to *'will'* so that it feels a bit more modern. It now becomes, *'I will not be afraid.'*

There is a lot of poetry in Psalm 56, and it seems to fit my theme quite well, so I'm also going to use verses 3 and 4 in the chorus:

> *When I'm afraid, I'll trust in you,* (Psalm 56:3)
> *My God, whose word I praise.* (Psalm 56:4)
> *For all my days, you'll be with me,* (Joshua 1:5-6)
> *I will not be afraid.* (Psalm 56:11)

5. Set It To Music

Now that you have the words you need music. If you are musical you can write the melody yourself, or if you know someone who is musical you can ask them to compose the tune for your hymn. Alternatively, if you aren't musical and you can't find anyone who is, you can pair your hymn with a tune that fits your lyrics. This is how many hymn writers used to work. They would write words to a pre-existing piece of music.

I haven't composed music for my hymn, but because it shares the same metre as *Amazing Grace* it could be sung to the same tune. It could also be sung to the tune of *While Shepherds Watched Their Flocks By Night, O Little Town of Bethlehem,* or even *The House Of The Rising Sun* by The Animals.

6. Name Your Hymn

Once you have written your hymn you should give it a title. Many hymns use the first line of the hymn as its title. Other hymns might use a line from the chorus. More modern worship songs often choose a title that isn't a direct lyric from the hymn but instead embodies the main theme of the song.

I'm going to name my hymn *I Will Not Fear*. It is the first line of my hymn, but also embodies the main theme of the hymn and is constantly repeated throughout.

What title are you going to give your hymn?

7. The Final Hymn

There are many other considerations that you might want to consider when writing your hymn. Such as: are you singing *about* God or *to* God? Is it a loud song of joy or a quiet song of reflection? Is the chorus a different tune to the verse? Does your hymn need a bridge? Seeing as this is a basic guide to writing your first hymn, you can address these questions at a later date. Right now the most important thing is just to have something written down. You can edit it and polish it later.

For now, let's look at the final version of my hymn *I Will Not Fear*. I've written two other verses, giving it a total of three verses and one chorus. The chorus will be sung at the end of each verse. At the end of each line I've included its biblical influence so that you can see how I have incorporated scripture into every line of the final song.

I hope that this inspires you to write your own hymns, and has shown you how accessible hymn-writing is. If you do write a hymn of your own please e-mail it to **hello@hymnsofnote.com**. I'd love to read it!

So, without further ado, here is *I Will Not Fear* :

I Will Not Fear

2021

Words

William Long

I will not fear, you're on my side, (Psalm 118:6)
My refuge from the storm. (Isaiah 25:4)
I will not fear, I am redeemed, (Isaiah 43:1)
You summoned me by name. (Isaiah 43:1)

When I'm afraid, I'll trust in you, (Psalm 56:3)
My God, whose word I praise. (Psalm 56:4)
For all my days, you'll be with me, (Joshua 1:5-6)
I will not be afraid. (Psalm 56:11)

I will not fear, nor be dismayed, (Isaiah 41:10)
You're fighting by my side (Deuteronomy 3:22)
I will not fear, but I will praise, (Psalm 56:3)
For you are God alone. (Isaiah 44:8)

I will not fear, you are my light, (Psalm 27:1)
The stronghold of my life. (Psalm 27:1)
I will not fear, your love abounds! (Psalm 86:15)
There is no fear in love. (1 John 4:18)

Bibliography

"Abide With Me (1914)." The Public Domain Review, publicdomainre-
    view.org/collection/abide-with-me-1914.

"Abide with Me: Fast Falls the Eventide." Hymnary.org,
    hymnary.org/text/abide_with_me_fast_falls_the_eventide.

Adey, Lionel. Hymns and the Christian "Myth". University of British Columbia Press,
    1988.

Aitken, Jonathan. John Newton: from Disgrace to Amazing Grace. Crossway Books, 2013.

Altobello, Brian. Into the Shadows Furious: the World War II Assault on New Georgia.
    Presidio Press, 2000.

"Amazing Grace! (How Sweet the Sound)." Hymnary.org,
    hymnary.org/text/amazing_grace_how_sweet_the_sound.

"And Can It Be, That I Should Gain?" Hymnary.org,
    hymnary.org/text/and_can_it_be_that_i_should_gain#tune.

Aðalsteinsson Jón Hnefill. Blót And Þing. The Function of the Tenth Century Goði. 1985.

Bales, Kevin. Disposable People: New Slavery in the Global Economy. University of Cali-
    fornia Press, 2012.

Ballard, Robert D., and Michael Hamilton Morgan. Collision with History: the Search for
    John F. Kennedy's PT 109. National Geographic Society, 2002.

Ballhorn, Egbert. Die O-Antiphonen: Israelgebet Der Kirche. Jahrbuch Für Liturgik Und
    Hymnologie. , 1998.

"Before the Throne of God Above." Hymnary.org,
    hymnary.org/text/before_the_throne_of_god_above_i_have_a_.

Bible Verses for The Lord Will Provide by John Newton, Blogger, 21 May 2020, scripture-
    and.blogspot.com/2020/05/bible-verses-for-lord-will-provide-by.html.

Bradbury, William B. Bradbury's Golden Chain and Shower for the Sabbath School. Hen-
    ry A. Brown, 1866.

Bradley, Ian C. The Daily Telegraph Book of Hymns. Continuum, 2006.

"Charles Albert Tindley." Hymnary.org,
> hymnary.org/person/Tindley_CA?tab=hymnals.

Charles S. Nutter: Hymn Writers of the Church - Christian Classics Ethereal Library,
> ccel.org/ccel/nutter/hymnwriters/hymnwriters.Tate_Nah.html.

Christensen, Camilla. "'Hear, Smith of the Heavens, What the Poet Asks': the Story of
> Kolbeinn Tumason and Heyr Himna Smiður." Legends of the North, leg-
> endsofthenorth.blogspot.com/2016/02/hear-smith-of-heavens-what-poet-asks.html.

Christian Singers of Germany. Hardpress Ltd, 2013.

Cottrill, Robert. "Today in 1933 – Charles Tindley Died." Wordwise Hymns, 5 May 2012,
> wordwisehymns.com/2010/07/26/today-in-1933-charles-albert-tindley-died/.

"Crown Him with Many Crowns - Lyrics, Hymn Meaning and Story." GodTube,
> www.godtube.com/popular-hymns/crown-him-with-many-crowns-lyrics-story-
> behind-hymn/.

"Crown Him with Many Crowns." Hymnary.org,
> hymnary.org/text/crown_him_with_many_crowns.

Donovan, Robert J. PT109: John F. Kennedy in World War II. McGraw-Hill, 2001.

Dunn, John. A Biography of John Newton. New Creation Teaching Ministry, 1970.

Dusevic, Tom. "A Friend in Deed." Time, 8 Aug. 2005.

Elkins, Yvonne Nannette. "What a Friend We Have in Jesus; The Story behind the
> Hymn." -, 31 Dec. 2020, www.hopeinthehealing.com/2020/03/24/what-a-friend-
> we-have-in-jesus-the-story-behind-the-hymn/.

ESV Student Study Bible: English Standard Version. Crossway, 2017.

Eve. "Frederick M. Lehman and 'The Love of God.'" West Park Baptist Church, 6 Feb.
> 2020, westpark-baptist.com/frederick-m-lehman/.

Eyerly, Sarah. "The Humble Origins of 'Silent Night'." The Conversation, 28 Apr. 2021,
> theconversation.com/the-humble-origins-of-silent-night-108653.

"Filter." CSUDH News, 2 May 2011, news.csudh.edu/hansonia-caldwellpresents-final-
> spiritual-concert/.

"Francis Rous." Hymnary.org, hymnary.org/person/Rous_F.

"Frederick M. Lehman." Hymnary.org, hymnary.org/person/Lehman_FM.

"Frederick Martin Lehman." WikiTree, 27 Aug. 2019, www.wikitree.com/wiki/Lehman-
> 981.

Gealy, Fred Daniel, et al. Companion to the Hymnal: a Handbook to the 1964 Methodist
> Hymnal. Abingdon, 1981.

"Great Is Thy Faithfulness." Hymnary.org,
> hymnary.org/text/great_is_thy_faithfulness_o_god_my_fathe.

Griffith, Stephen. "FolkSongIndex.com." FolkSongIndexcom,
www.stephengriffith.com/folksongindex/i-shall-not-be-moved/.

Gunnell, Terry. The Origins of Drama in Scandinavia. D.S. Brewer, 2008.

Hawn . "History of Hymns: 'Crown Him with Many Crowns.'" Discipleship Ministries, 14
June 2013, www.umcdiscipleship.org/resources/history-of-hymns-crown-him-with-
many-crowns.

Hawn, C. Michael. "History of Hymns: 'Great Is Thy Faithfulness.'" Discipleship Ministries, 23 Aug. 2013, www.umcdiscipleship.org/resources/history-of-hymns-great-is-
thy-faithfulness.

Hawn. "History of Hymns: Easter Celebration Hymn Transcends Time, Cultures." Discipleship Ministries, 31 May 2013, www.umcdiscipleship.org/resources/history-of-
hymns-easter-celebration-hymn-transcends-time-cultures-1.

Hawn. "History of Hymns: 'Nothing Between.'" Discipleship Ministries, 20 June 2013,
www.umcdiscipleship.org/resources/history-of-hymns-nothing-between.

Henh, Jonathan. "History of Hymns: 'Man of Sorrows! What a Name.'" Discipleship Ministries, 14 Apr. 2016, www.umcdiscipleship.org/resources/history-of-hymns-man-of-
sorrows-what-a-name.

"Henry Francis Lyte." Hymnary.org, hymnary.org/person/Lyte_HF.

"History of Hymns: 'Where Shall My Wondering Soul Begin'." Discipleship Ministries, 10
Oct. 2019, www.umcdiscipleship.org/articles/history-of-hymns-where-shall-my-
wondering-soul-begin.

"History of Hymns: 'And Can It Be That I Should Gain.'" Discipleship Ministries, 30 May
2018, www.umcdiscipleship.org/resources/history-of-hymns-and-can-it-be-that-i-
should-gain.

"History of Hymns: 'O Come, O Come, Emmanuel.'" Discipleship Ministries, 20 May
2013, www.umcdiscipleship.org/resources/history-of-hymns-o-come-o-come-
emmanuel.

"History of Hymns: 'Praise to the Lord, the Almighty.'" Discipleship Ministries, 21 June
2013, www.umcdiscipleship.org/resources/history-of-hymns-praise-to-the-lord-the-
almighty.

Hove, Duane T. American Warriors: Five Presidents in the Pacific Theater of World War
II. Burd Street Press, 2003.

Hyles, Jack. "The Story Behind The Psalms." The Story Behind The Psalms - by Dr Jack
Hyles, www.fbbc.com/messages/hyles_psalms.htm.

"I Shall Not Be Moved." Hymnary.org,
hymnary.org/text/jesus_keeps_forever_i_shall_not_be_moved.

"Jesus Loves Me, This I Know." Hymnary.org,
    hymnary.org/text/jesus_loves_me_this_i_know_for_the_bible.

JOHN NEWTON, www.paperlesshymnal.com/tph/stories/johnnewton/index.htm.

John Newton: Olney Hymns - Christian Classics Ethereal Library,
    www.ccel.org/ccel/newton/olneyhymns.Book1.GEN.h1_7.html.

Johnson, James Weldon, and J. Rosamond Johnson. The Books of American Negro Spirit-
    uals. Da Capo Press, 2002.

Jones, Ralph H. Charles Albert Tindley, Prince of Preachers. Abingdon Press, 1982.

"The Journal Of Charles Wesley." The Wesley Center Online: The Journal Of Charles
    Wesley: May 1 - August 31, 1738, wesley.nnu.edu/charles-wesley/the-journal-of-
    charles-wesley-1707-1788/the-journal-of-charles-wesley-may-1-august-31-1738.

Julian, John. Dictionary of Hymnology. 1957.

Kauflin, Bob. "A Hymn for Ordinary Christians - Great Is Thy Faithfulness." Worship
    Matters, 3 Aug. 2009, worshipmatters.com/2009/08/03/a-hymn-for-ordinary-
    christians-great-is-thy-faithfulness/.

Kidson, Frank. "Church and Organ Music: 'Abide With Me'"." The Musical Times, 1 Jan.
    1908, pp. 24–25.

Lamport, Mark A., et al. Hymns and Hymnody: Historical and Theological Introductions.
    Cascade Books, 2019.

Larrea, Beñat Elortza. "Medieval Scandinavia: The Rise and Fall of the Icelandic Com-
    monwealth." Medievalists.net, 19 Sept. 2020,
    www.medievalists.net/2020/09/medieval-icelandic-commonwealth/.

Lewis, Frank. Seller Image Essex and Sugar : Historic and Other Connections / by Frank
    Lewis ; with a Foreword by Lord Lyle of Westbourne. Phillimore, 1976.

Literacy, umich.edu/~ece/student_projects/print_culture/literacy.html

Little, Patrick. Oliver Cromwell: New Perspectives. Palgrave MacMillan, 2008.

"The Lord Will Provide." Hymnary.org,
    hymnary.org/text/though_troubles_assail_and_dangers_affri.

"The Lord's My Shepherd." Hymnary.org,
    hymnary.org/text/the_lords_my_shepherd_ill_not_want_rous.

"The Love of God Is Greater Far." Hymnstudiesblog, 20 Nov. 2017, hymnstud-
    iesblog.wordpress.com/2017/11/20/the-love-of-god-is-greater-far/.

"The Love of God Song Story." Redeemer, Redeemer, 27 Oct. 2016,
    www.redeemerrr.org/blog/2016/10/26/anchored-song-stories-pt2-by-chris-
    mallonee.

"The Love of God." Hymnary.org, hymnary.org/text/the_love_of_god_is_greater_far.

Martin, Bernard. John Newton: a Biography. Heinemann, 1950.

Masters, Peter. Men of Purpose. The Wakeman Trust, 2013.

McCann, Forrest Mason. Hymns and History: an Annotated Survey of Sources. ACU Press, 1997.

Morgan, Robert J. Then Sings My Soul. Thomas Nelson, 2011.

Morgan, Robert J. Then Sings My Soul: 150 of the World's Greatest Hymn Stories. T. Nelson, 2004.

Nahum Tate, www.nndb.com/people/448/000098154/.

"Neale, John Mason (NL836JM)." A Cambridge Alumni Database, University of Cambridge, venn.lib.cam.ac.uk/ .

Newton, John, and Dennis R. Hillman. Out of the Depths. Kregel Publications, 2003.

"Nothing Between." Hymnary.org, hymnary.org/text/nothing_between_my_soul_and_my_savior.

"O Come O Come Emmanuel." Dominican Friars Province of St. Joseph, 3 Nov. 2016, opeast.org/2011/12/o-come-o-come-emmanuel/ .

"O Come, O Come, Emmanuel." Hymnary.org, hymnary.org/text/o_come_o_come_emmanuel_and_ransom.

Osbeck, Kenneth W. 101 Hymn Stories: the Inspiring Stories behind 101 Favorite Hymns. Kregel, 2012.

Piper, John. "Ambushing Satan with Song." Desiring God, 9 July 2021, www.desiringgod.org/messages/ambushing-satan-with-song.

"Praise to the Lord, the Almighty." Hymnary.org, hymnary.org/text/praise_to_the_lord_the_almighty_the_king.

Psalm 16:8 Commentaries: I Have Set the LORD Continually before Me; Because He Is at My Right Hand, I Will Not Be Shaken., biblehub.com/commentaries/psalms/16-8.htm.

Rainer, Melanie. "Abide with Me." She Reads Truth, 22 July 2020, shereadstruth.com/abide-with-me/ .

"Revelation 19:12." BibleRef.com, www.bibleref.com/Revelation/19/Revelation-19-12.html.

Romain, St. "History of Hymns: 'Abide with Me.'" Discipleship Ministries, 21 June 2013, www.umcdiscipleship.org/resources/history-of-hymns-abide-with-me.

Royals Gather For Easter Service. 8 Apr. 2012, nationalfeeds.newsquest.co.uk/news/national/9638026.royals-gather-for-easter-service/ .

"Silent Night, Holy Night." Hymnary.org,
hymnary.org/text/silent_night_holy_night_all_is_calm_all.

"Slavery Today " Free the Slaves." Free the Slaves, www.freetheslaves.net/our-model-for-freedom/slavery-today/.

"Slavery, Slave, Transatlantic Trade, Africa, Human Trafficking, Human Rights, Slave Route." United Nations, United Nations,
www.un.org/en/events/slaveryremembranceday/background.shtml.

Smith, George, et al. The Dictionary of National Biography. Oxford University Press, 1998.

Spener, David. We Shall Not Be Moved/No Nos Moverán: Biography of a Song of Struggle. Temple University Press, 2016.

Spielberg, Steven, director. Indiana Jones and the Raiders of the Lost Ark. Paramount, 1981.

Tabb, Kristin. "Worship in Your Waiting." Desiring God, 9 July 2021,
www.desiringgod.org/articles/worship-in-your-waiting.

"Thine Is the Glory." Hymnary.org,
hymnary.org/text/thine_is_the_glory_risen_conquering.

Tumason, and Anon. "Heyr, Himna Smiður (Hear, Smith of the Heavens): Song Texts, Lyrics & Translations." Oxford Lieder, www.oxfordlieder.co.uk/song/3645.

"Tune: [Man of Sorrows, What a Name]." Hymnary.org,
hymnary.org/tune/man_of_sorrows_what_a_name_bliss.

"Um Hólaskóla Hinn Forna Eftir GÍSLA JÓNSSON Jón Ögmundarson (1052¬1121) Var." Mbl.is, Mbl.is, 4 Dec. 2002, www.mbl.is/greinasafn/grein/125958/.

Watson, J. R. An Annotated Anthology of Hymns. Oxford University Press, 2002.

Wedgwood, C. V. The King's Peace, 1637-1641 / by C. V. Wedgwood. Collins, 1955.

Wells, Robert V. Life Flows on in Endless Song: Folk Songs and American History. University of Illinois Press, 2009.

"What a Friend We Have in Jesus." Hymnary.org,
hymnary.org/text/what_a_friend_we_have_in_jesus_all_our_s.

"While Shepherds Watched Their Flocks." The Hymns and Carols of Christmas,
www.hymnsandcarolsofchristmas.com/Hymns_and_Carols/while_shepherds_watched_their_fl.htm.

White, Rhonda. "I Shall Not Be Moved - Are You Planted Deeply in Your Christian Faith?" HerChristianhome, 10 Oct. 2018, herchristianhome.com/i-shall-not-be-i-shall-not-be-moved-are-you-planted-deeply/.

Wilson, Chris. "The Most Popular Christmas Song Ever." Time, Time, 2 Dec. 2014,
    time.com/3613551/christmas-song/.

Yarbrough, Alan. "Before the Throne of God Above." Medium, Reflections on Music,
    Worship, and Spiritual Formation, 21 July 2017, medium.com/congregational-
    song/hymn-reflection-before-the-throne-of-god-above-9e2e459cb840.

Young, Carlton R., et al. The Canterbury Dictionary of Hymnology. Canterbury Press,
    2013.

"'Nothing Between.'" Hymnstudiesblog, 23 Nov. 2009, hymnstud-
    iesblog.wordpress.com/2009/11/23/quotnothing-betweenquot/.

About The Author

William Long was born in 1987. He grew up in Hertford, UK, and has a BA in filmmaking from the University of the Arts London. He has played the guitar since he was five years old (because his parents wouldn't let him have a Gameboy) and plays in a band at Hertford Baptist Church, where he occasionally leads worship. He has volunteered as a Young Life leader, and as a youth group leader for his church, for over ten years. He now works full time as a film editor and has edited three feature films. He has published a feature article on film postproduction in *The Digital Video Book* for Future PLC. He has also written scripts for animated short films, which have been shown at festivals around the world. In his free time, he likes to make games and write stories. He published his first book, *Hymns Of Note*, in 2020. He lives in Stanstead Abbotts with his wife Agnes, and two Khaki Campbell ducks called Chester and Marjory.

You can see more of his work at:

www.hymnsofnote.com
www.longfilms.co.uk
www.longgames.co.uk